Yes, You Can Get Pregnant

Also by Aimee E. Raupp, MS, LAc

Chill Out and Get Healthy:
Live Clean to Be Strong and Stay Sexy

Yes, You Can Get Pregnant

Natural Ways to Improve Your Fertility Now and into Your 40s

Aimee E. Raupp, MS, LAc

demosHEALTH

NEW YORK

Visit our website at www.demoshealth.com

ISBN: 978-1-936303-69-4
e-book ISBN: 978-1-61705-217-0

Acquisitions Editor: Julia Pastore
Compositor: diacriTech

Medical information provided by Demos Health, in the absence of a visit with a health care professional, must be considered as an educational service only. This book is not designed to replace a physician's independent judgment about the appropriateness or risks of a procedure or therapy for a given patient. Our purpose is to provide you with information that will help you make your own health care decisions.

The information and opinions provided here are believed to be accurate and sound, based on the best judgment available to the authors, editors, and publisher, but readers who fail to consult appropriate health authorities assume the risk of injuries. The publisher is not responsible for errors or omissions. The editors and publisher welcome any reader to report to the publisher any discrepancies or inaccuracies noticed.

Library of Congress Cataloging-in-Publication Data
Raupp, Aimee E.
  Yes, you can get pregnant : natural ways to improve your fertility now and into your 40s / Aimee E. Raupp, MS, LAc.
    pages cm
  Includes bibliographical references and index.
  ISBN 978-1-936303-69-4
  1. Infertility, Female–Diet therapy–Recipes. 2. Conception–Popular works. I. Title.
  RG201.R38 2014
  618.1'78—dc23

2014000934

Special discounts on bulk quantities of Demos Health books are available to corporations, professional associations, pharmaceutical companies, health care organizations, and other qualifying groups. For details, please contact:

Special Sales Department
Demos Medical Publishing, LLC
11 West 42nd Street, 15th Floor
New York, NY 10036
Phone: 800-532-8663 or 212-683-0072
Fax: 212-941-7842
E-mail: specialsales@demosmedpub.com

Printed in the United States of America by McNaughton & Gunn.
14 15 16 17 18 / 5 4 3 2 1

This book is dedicated to YOU.
May YOU realize YOUR power and allow all that
YOU desire in life to come to YOU.

Tenacity never killed the cat
In fact, it made him fat
Not in girth
But in self-worth
Keep on dreaming
Keep on trying
Keep on going—til you find it
To squeaky wheels on endless tracks
To college kids in baseball caps
To YOU—to prove that we still have
Tenacity and Happy Cats
—Harry F. Raupp

Contents

Part III: More Fertility-Enhancing Tips and Ways to Overcome Common Fertility Challenges

Author's Note

All names and identifying characteristics of my clients have been changed to protect their privacy.

Preface

Why This Book Is For You

Are you worried about your ability to get pregnant?

Are you obsessed with how many eggs your ovaries have left?

Did someone tell you that women over the age of 35 have a harder time getting pregnant and now you're beyond stressed out?

Have you read everything on the Internet about improving your fertility and you don't know where to start?

If you answered yes to any one of those questions, *Yes, You Can Get Pregnant* is for you. Whether you are single and 37 and want to preserve your fertility because you know one day you will meet your mate and want to make babies, or you are 28 and just off the pill and want to get your reproductive system in optimal health, or you are 33 and coupled and just beginning to think about having a baby, or you are 39 and currently trying to get pregnant or have been struggling with conceiving, or you are 43 and headed into your first round of Western fertility treatments, *Yes, You Can Get Pregnant* is for you. This book is for *any* woman of *any* reproductive age who wants to improve her fertility. *Yes, You Can Get Pregnant* is the complete holistic guide to getting your health and your fertility in the best shape possible so you can get pregnant when you want to.

Some of you may be just beginning to think about having babies; some of you may have one child and want a second; some of you may be knee-deep in infertility treatments, pumped up on hormones, and pulling your hair out. No matter where you are on the path of having a baby, this book will help you. *Yes, You Can Get Pregnant* will take you on an uplifting tour of your baby-making machinery: your female reproductive system, including your uterus, ovaries, fallopian tubes, and cervix. We will cover topics from eating for optimal egg quality to what environmental toxins you need to avoid, from orgasms to follicle-stimulating hormone, from endometriosis to emotional breakdowns, from miscarriages to bed rest, from a great sex life to a forced-honey-I'm-ovulating-NOW sex life. We'll get into the emotional aspect of infertility and shift your focus from infertility back to fertility. With my clinical expertise and my extensive Eastern and Western medical knowledge combined with the most recent scientific research and some valuable insight from doctors specializing in reproductive medicine, you will get your health and your fertility on track.

The fertility rejuvenation protocol laid out in *Yes, You Can Get Pregnant* is a lifestyle plan that is easy to follow, will make you feel and look better, improve your overall health, and markedly enhance your fertility. You'll be able to start applying the practical diet and lifestyle tips to promote fertility and balance your hormones immediately as well as the many techniques to reduce stress and anxiety, boost your immune system, and improve your emotional well-being. Here's the key, though: all of the information in this book must be implemented into your life for your fertility to truly be rejuvenated. I encourage you to read this book front to back—in the order it is laid out—and to *follow every part* of the fertility rejuvenation protocol. Embrace *all* of the material in *Yes, You Can Get Pregnant* and rejuvenate your life, your health, and your fertility.

Keep in mind, the information in this book is not a substitute for medical care and shouldn't be used as such. I encourage you to work with a team of health care providers, both Western and Eastern. With this approach, you will find your best solutions for rejuvenating your fertility.

I welcome you to turn the page and get started!

Introduction

Sarah walked into my office for her weekly acupuncture appointment looking worn-out and pale from her most recent miscarriage. As she entered, tears welled up in her eyes. I met her at the door with a hug.

"Aimee, this sucks," she said, as she sat down on the treatment table, clearly exhausted.

Nodding in agreement, I said, "It does. What did your fertility doctor say?"

Sighing, she said, "He still thinks we have some time to decide on next steps. Do you think we should go straight to in vitro?" (She was referring to in vitro fertilization, or IVF.)

Sarah will be 37 years old in four months. She just got married a year ago and has become pregnant twice since the wedding. She lost both pregnancies at nine weeks. It's been a rough year for her and her husband. Sarah came to me as a new patient after her first miscarriage. The tissue sample from her first dilation and curettage (D&C) did not reveal anything significant as to why Sarah had miscarried. After her second miscarriage, the D&C showed a genetic abnormality, meaning something was chromosomally wrong with the embryo.

"How are you recovering from this last D&C?"

"I've been bleeding on and off for the last two weeks. The cramping the first two days was intense. All looked fine when my doctor did the ultrasound yesterday. Today, I saw some egg-white-ish mucus. Do you think I'm ovulating? Should we be trying right now?"

"I think you should wait until you get another period as your uterus, and your heart, are not yet recovered from this last miscarriage and D&C. You can try again next cycle. How are you and Seth doing?"

Sarah took a deep breath. "Yea, my heart is definitely broken right now. Seth is real sad too, but he keeps reminding me that no matter what, we are just so lucky to have each other. I just keep thinking about that time when we got pregnant when we were first dating." Seth and Sarah dated for two years before they got married and less than two months into their relationship, they got pregnant. They decided not to keep the baby.

"Sarah, you can't do that to yourself. I know it's hard, but you have to believe that you are where you're supposed to be. You two are in such a strong place now as a couple."

"I know." She started to cry. I gently put my hand on her wrist and felt her weak pulse. In Traditional Oriental Medicine (TOM), we use the pulse to diagnose and determine the best acupuncture points to treat our patients. However, it is not only diagnostic to feel the pulse; a simple touch can also be comforting to patients.

"And what do you guys think about the next steps?"

"I don't know, Aim. I'm getting worried. I'm obviously infertile. I guess we have to do in vitro. What do you think?"

"Whoa. 'Obviously infertile'? Sarah, you've just had two miscarriages back to back. I know that's not what you wanted, but the truth is you *are* fertile and you *can* get pregnant. In the world of fertility, the fact that you can get pregnant is huge. What is most important, is that you remain fertility focused, *not* infertility focused. Whether you decide to continue trying naturally or do IVF you need to *first have the belief in your body and its ability to get pregnant and carry a pregnancy to term*. I have seen this situation on a number of occasions, and I'd suggest you continue to try on your own for another three months. However, I can't stress enough the importance that you let go of this belief that your body is infertile. That belief is not serving you; rather, it's making you believe that there is something wrong, that you are broken. The mind is powerful. Rather than focusing on something being wrong, shift your focus to the exciting possibility that this is all going to work out and you are going to get pregnant and stay pregnant and have a healthy child, very soon."

"I know. It's hard. Everywhere I go, I hear about someone else dealing with infertility," Sarah said, with a crack in her voice. "I'm just scared that now I'm that girl too. Now, I'm the infertile one. I'm not getting any younger and everything I read online talks about how the older I get, the more common miscarriages are."

"I hear you. I know it's hard. But truthfully, you are getting pregnant. Now we just need the next one to stick. In TOM we see a strong correlation between one's emotional state and one's physical health. If you don't believe in your body's ability to get pregnant and stay pregnant, if you are constantly sending negative, worrisome messages to your uterus, it's going to be hard to get past these miscarriages and onto a healthy pregnancy. Don't give up your power here. This is your body and your fertility. Believe in your fertility. Remember at our first appointment when I asked you whether or not you thought you would birth your own children? What was your answer to me?"

Sarah started to cry, "It was a yes. I really did believe it then."

I softly squeezed her wrist and said, "I know it's not easy right now, but try to get back to that place of believing. When I met you, you just knew you were fertile; you were so sure of your fertility. Sure, that first miscarriage wasn't fun, and the second one sucked. But you *are* getting pregnant and you will carry a pregnancy to term. Know that."

She nodded, "I'm going to try. You are right. I need to believe in my body."

"Yes, the first step is believing. Then, continue with the dietary changes and lifestyle modifications you've been following along with the acupuncture, and tracking your ovulation and seeing your fertility doctor, and I really do think you can do this. If you're not pregnant in three more months, then we can talk more about the next steps. But, I can't stress it enough: before we go any further, you need to get back to believing in your body. Get off those online infertility forums that talk about all the reproductive problems out there. All that negativity isn't good for you."

Sarah laughed through her tears and nodded in agreement. "Sounds like a plan, Aimee." I gave her a tissue, silently put her acupuncture needles in, made sure she was warm, dimmed the light, and left her to relax during her treatment.

Just as I walked out of Sarah's treatment room, I was greeted by my next patient, Mindy. Mindy is a 33-year-old pediatric nurse, whom I see twice a month. She has been a patient of mine for three years. She first started seeing me for migraines, and over the years we have worked through bouts of anxiety attacks, cystic acne, insomnia, a near divorce, and premenstrual migraines. Nine months ago, Mindy went off the pill after being on it for 17 years. She is eager to get pregnant.

"Hey there," I said as I show her into her treatment room.

With an irritated look on her face, Mindy sat up on the treatment table and said, "I still haven't gotten my period. I took a pregnancy test this morning and it was negative. I called the fertility center to make an appointment. I can't take this anymore. Aimee, we've been trying for nine months and I'm not pregnant."

"Mindy, you know I'm coming from a loving place when I say this, as you're a nurse and I know you know the basics of reproduction just as well as I do. You know that you can't count the months, you need to count the menstrual cycles. Since you went off the pill nine months ago, you have had six months without a period, and it was only the last two months when you had what seemed to be a normal period. Those first six months don't count as you weren't menstruating. Now that you're menstruating again, your body does seem to be regulating itself. Our job here is to get your period coming regularly *and* your body to be ovulating each month. Only then can you get pregnant."

Mindy let out a big sigh, "I know. You're right. It just feels like we've been trying to conceive for so long. That pill screwed me up."

"The science shows it can take six to nine months to restore a normal ovulatory cycle after going off the pill. Six months after you went off the pill, you got your first period. This is a good sign. Your hormonal system is balancing out."

"I'm just really frustrated, Aimee. I want to get pregnant *now*."

"I know. Let's use some perspective: your period has come the last two months, and you ovulated the last two months. Pregnancy is bound to happen. You are young, you are healthy. Have faith in your body and the lifestyle changes you are making to improve your fertility. The way I see it, ever since you changed your diet, went off the pill, and started meditating daily, your hormones have really balanced out: you're getting fairly regular periods, you aren't getting any premenstrual migraines like you were when you were on the pill, you don't have any more hormonal acne, and you're finally ovulating again. Those are all good signs."

Mindy lay back on the treatment table and closed her eyes. "I know. Honestly, it's just hard being at work around all those little kids when I want one of my own so badly."

"I can't imagine. That must be hard," I said, as I touched her wrist and felt her pulse. "You are going to have your own little one soon enough."

"I will, right? I mean my period did come pretty much on time the last two months, and you're right, I haven't had a migraine since I went off the pill."

"Yes, keep seeing all the positive changes your body has gone through recently. Also, I want you to stop telling yourself you've been trying for nine months because the first six didn't count. You have had two fairly normal menstrual cycles and therefore have had two attempts at pregnancy, not nine."

With a big sigh, Mindy just nodded her head, yes.

"Mindy, let's stay the course. Your body is balancing out after 17 years of taking the pill. That's a long time and you need to give your body time to recalibrate more. It will. It has been recalibrating already and you will get pregnant soon."

Mindy looked at me as if she finally heard me, "You're right. Thanks for the pep talk, Aim. I needed it."

"Any time, Mindy. That's my job. I only see the fertility and the wellness in my patients. I want you to see only your fertility and wellness too."

Day in and day out, I see scores of different versions of both these stories in my clinic. I see women who are over-the-moon happy that they are pregnant, women who are vomiting every day with morning sickness, women who are obsessively tracking their ovulation, women who have just delivered their beautiful baby after two years of trying to conceive, women who no longer enjoy nor want sex because each time they have it they wonder, "is this the month

I'll get pregnant?" I see women who are scared to become mothers, women who are aching to become mothers, women who have just undergone their first, second, and third IVF, and women considering adoption, donor eggs, or donor sperm. I've worked with women who have lost babies at 20 weeks, women who are on bed rest for the last half of their pregnancies, and women with rare genetic disorders who had to terminate their pregnancies. After almost 10 years of treating fertility patients in my clinic, I've seen it all. No matter what situation I see, my job is the same: *I am here to help you believe in your body and your fertility again*. Yes, I am also here to give you advice that will help you get pregnant, remain pregnant to term, have a smooth and easy delivery, and keep you sane through it all. However, *first and foremost, I am here to bring your focus away from infertility and back to fertility*.

What I see most frequently in my clinical practice is how a lot of hurt, fear, trauma, anxiety, and sorrow impede a woman's ability to get pregnant. Just like I did with Sarah and Mindy, in this book I will gently coach you back to believing in your abundant fertility. I will cheer you on while you shift from seeing all the things that are going wrong to all the positive improvements in your health that ultimately are improving your fertility.

Before we get into the how, I want to plant this mental seed: *you have the power to change your health and improve your fertility*. From this moment forward, I am going to ask you to stop believing in the *in*ability, the *in*capability, the *in*conceivability, or the *in*fertility of your body. Instead, I want you to believe in the capabilities, the abilities, and the fertile possibilities of your body.

Say it to yourself right now: "I have the power to change MY health and improve MY fertility." This is your new mantra. Own it. Love it. Believe it. Throughout this book, I will be pointing out the places where you should be repeating this mantra, lovingly, to yourself. Beyond anything I am going to tell you, the most important fertility tool you possess is *your ability to believe in your body and its fertility*. YOU have the power here and YOU can improve your fertility. The rest of the information in this book will definitely help you whether or not you believe, but believing will get you there faster. So take the first step and believe in your body. I know you can do it, and I'm going to be your biggest cheerleader.

Before we begin, let me tell you a bit about me, your new cheerleader: I have been in clinical practice for 10 years as a licensed acupuncturist, Chinese herbalist, and a practitioner of TOM with a specialty in women's wellness and fertility. For most people, when they think of an acupuncturist they think of needles. Most acupuncturists do use needles to restore health to their patients; however, there is a lot more to TOM than needles. TOM is a 5000-year-old medical system that originated in China as a natural healing method. In stark contrast to Western medicine, TOM takes a holistic approach to health: the TOM practitioner focuses on the root causes of illness, not just on the symptoms. TOM takes into account every aspect of every person—body, mind, spirit, and emotions—and works to encourage the body's innate ability to heal itself. With those tenets in mind, when it comes to helping my patients achieve optimal health and fertility and ultimately get pregnant, I not only use acupuncture, but I also employ several techniques including Chinese herbal remedies, science-backed lifestyle changes, and nutritional advice. I have brought all of this expertise to bear in the creation of the rejuvenation plan in this book. You'll learn how to:

- get your reproductive system, specifically your uterus—known as your "child's palace" in TOM—in the most fertile shape possible;
- get your premenstrual symptoms and other hormonally related issues such as premenstrual migraines, raging emotions, acne, breast tenderness, bloating, vicious menstrual cramps, irregular periods, and ovulation under control;
- eat optimally for exceptional health and fertility;
- boost your immune system to manage any potentially undiagnosed autoimmune diseases such as autoimmune thyroid disease (AITD) and celiac disease (CD), both of which can pose serious threats to your health and your fertility;
- eliminate the harmful environmental toxins from your life that have been scientifically proven to harm fertility (yours and your man's);
- get you back to a place of believing in your power to improve your health and your fertility and encourage you to let go of the worrisome burdens you are putting on your body and your fertility.

And, most importantly, I will guide you on how to put all of this together into a simple health- and fertility-enhancing lifestyle over-haul that you will feel good about. If this sounds like a lot, take a deep breath and know that I am here to coach you, as I do all of my patients, back into a place of believing in your body and its ability to heal and balance itself. *Yes, You Can Get Pregnant* will not only con-vince you that you have the power to improve your health and your fertility, but it will also cheeringly show you how to do it.

I know that not all of you reading this book are like Sarah or Mindy. Some of you have been dealing with trying to get pregnant for years, some for months; some of you are just kind of, sort of think-ing about it. For ALL of you, one very important point must be made clear before reading any further: never doubt your body and its ability to get pregnant. Rather, you should have such a strong belief in your body that you are sure of its ability to conceive. If that sounds like an impossibility to you right now, it's time again for you to repeat your new favorite mantra:

> I have the power to change MY health and improve MY fertility.

When you read that you have the power, that I want you to believe in your body and be confident in your baby-making health and your ability to become a mother, I understand that may be a stretch to believe in *right now*, especially if you've been trying to conceive for some time. I know that dealing with being "fertility challenged" is mercurial, to say the least. But it is my hope that by the time you finish this book you will feel uplifted, empowered, and resolute in your ability to improve your fertility and become a mother.

I believe your uterus wants to do its job. I believe in the fertil-ity in all of you. I believe in your ability to improve your health and your fertility. I am not denying that some women have real fertility issues and are having a harder time getting pregnant than others. I am aware that there are age-related fertility challenges that some women are facing. I am positive that the emotional and physical stress we are experiencing, certain foods we are eating, and the toxins in our environment that we are exposed to are all hurting our health and our fertility. This book is full of pertinent information that will help you work out all those tangible kinks. But, before we go any further, *I need you to believe in your fertility more than you don't believe in it, otherwise my ability to help you is hindered.*

I mean this from a real sincere, heart-to-heart place. It is my hope that this book not only will give you valuable information but also will inspire you to return to having faith in your body, your fertility, and your uterus. Working on freeing yourself from emotional burdens is just as important as deciding to follow the diet in this book. When you work on both the emotional and the physical aspects, together, your power over improving your health and your fertility will be immense. I am officially telling you: YOU have the power to improve your health and your fertility. It is in YOUR hands.

Now, turn the page, dig in, and let's talk about my least favorite word.

Yes, You Can Get Pregnant

Part I
You Have the Power

1
My Least Favorite Word: Shifting from Being Infertility Focused to Fertility Focused

My least favorite word is *infertility*. It's just such an ugly word. It reeks of negativity. It oozes failure. Hearing it hurts my heart and my uterus. I'm sure it hurts yours too. The word infertility takes away some of the power we have over our health and our fertility. And, as I said in the "Introduction," I am here to remind you that *you have the power over your fertility*. Just because someone told you that women over age 35 or women who have "old eggs" have a harder time getting pregnant doesn't mean that's you. It is my belief that talking about infertility, discussing it, telling stories about it, reading about it, focusing upon it, leads to more and more of a belief that you will be or are infertile. Each time you say that word, it removes a little of the possibility that everything is going exactly as it should be going and that your body has the innate ability to be healthy and conceive a child. So let's make a pact right now: no more of that word! Rather, let's shift our perspective to fertility. You are not "infertile"; your insides just need a little fertility enhancement or your lady parts need some fertility rejuvenation. None of which means that you're broken or that you can't get to where you want to be, which is brimming, overflowing, and abundant with pregnancy.

I've got a message for you: you have much more control over your health and fertility than you currently believe. Your health and your fertility are in *your* power. I'm here to encourage you to exercise that power. My job is to help you get to that place where you believe in the never-been-broken wholeness of your body again. My mission is to empower you with the tools that can help you shift your health and ultimately your fertility from a place of doubt to a place of hope, from a place of "I'm not sure" to a place of "YES, I CAN," from a place of uncertainty to a place of enormous fertile possibility. You have so much more power than you know. You have the power to improve your fertility.

First, we need to touch upon a very important topic that is at the crux of your fertility: your belief about your fertility.

Shifting from Being Infertility Focused to Fertility Focused

A day in my clinic is filled with every emotional extreme you can imagine: celebrations to crushing blows. We celebrate when a 40-year-old woman who, after seven years of trying to get pregnant and incessant fertility clinic visits, finally gets a positive pregnancy test. We celebrate when a 36-year-old woman makes it through her 20th week of pregnancy, as her last two pregnancies spontaneously aborted at 18 weeks of gestation. We celebrate when a 43-year-old woman gets pregnant naturally after two failed in vitro fertilization (IVF) procedures. We celebrate when a woman who after three years of trying to get pregnant realizes she's always wanted to adopt a beautiful baby.

Also, in a typical day in my practice, there are the moments of devastation. We are crushed when the third IVF didn't work for a 27-year-old woman and she feels hopeless. We cry when a 33-year-old woman has to terminate her pregnancy due to a previously unknown and rare genetic disorder. We are heartbroken when a 30-year-old woman who is trying to get pregnant discovers she has cervical cancer and needs a complete hysterectomy.

There are happy dances right in the waiting room of my office and high fives; there are endless tears and relentless doctor's visits;

there are a good amount of angry fits; and there are a lot of hopeful moments. Happily, for most all the women in my practice, there is at some point a positive-pregnancy-pee-stick-in-hand celebration; even the woman with cervical cancer went on to have two children via surrogacy.

Being fertility challenged is insane and erratic and heartbreaking, and something I wish no woman should ever have to endure. But what all this starts with is a woman coming into my office seeking help in becoming pregnant because somewhere along the way she began thinking, or she was told, or she indeed has had a difficult time conceiving. Whether that belief began when her doctor told her she would have a hard time, or when her best friend had trouble getting pregnant right away, or when she read about the difficulties a certain celebrity had while trying to conceive, the woman coming into my office formed a belief that she, too, was going to have difficulty. I'm not saying the belief is *incorrect*, but I am saying that the belief doesn't serve my patients nor does it serve you. By serving you I mean, it doesn't help you in this process, it doesn't make you feel good, it doesn't fill you with optimism; rather, it only serves to make you feel inadequate and fearful. Worse, it feeds the I'm-not-fertile belief inside of you and becomes a self-fulfilled prophecy.

Now I am encouraging you to form an I AM FERTILE belief, because that belief serves your fertility for the better. As I always say to my patients: there is so much good that comes from being optimistic. Optimism brings joy and hope into your heart and into your uterus. When you are trying to conceive, optimism serves you. Hope serves you. Believing in your fertility serves you.

For a woman who wants to have a child, the prospect of not getting pregnant when she wants to is beyond scary. Hope is hard to hold onto when you're fishing through all of the information on the Internet about improving your fertility. The information you come across when researching fertility can be not only terrifying but overwhelming, not to mention often misleading and not necessarily based on any real science. Blindly heading into the world of fertility clinics and assisted reproductive medicine can be daunting, exhausting, and take all of the sexy fun out of making babies. So I am telling you right now: stop reading stories about strangers on the Internet. Stop believing all the scary tales. Stop looking to your best friends to determine how your body may be broken. Start having hope. Start believing that you have power over your health and your fertility. When you do that, you shift your focus from lacking fertility to having fertility and you take back power. Even if you are fertility challenged at the moment, focus on having fertility and not on the lack of it. Start believing in your ability to shift your health, your fertility, and your mindset. You can do it.

Take a moment right now and repeat your new mantra:
I have the power to change MY health and improve
MY fertility.

Of course, I'm not saying it's easy living surrounded by the media, the Internet, our doctors, our mothers, and our friends, all of whom are talking about the lack of fertility. You can't avoid the fact that, according to the Centers for Disease Control (CDC), over seven million women and their partners are dealing with fertility issues. It's no wonder that the western world is infertility focused. Infertility (and this is the last time I will use that word in this book) as defined by the World Health Organization and the Mayo Clinic is: "a disease or condition of the reproductive system often diagnosed after a couple has one year of unprotected, well-timed intercourse or if the woman suffers from multiple miscarriages. If a woman is over the age of 35, the time of trying to conceive is reduced to 6 months. Infertility can be male or female related."

Let's break this down: so that's *one year* of *well-timed sex*. However, one year should really be stated as 12 menstrual cycles, which for some women can be longer or shorter than one year. Well-timed sex means the couple is having sex on or before (preferably before) ovulation actually occurs (more on the details of timing sex in chapter 2). These two points are key, as the timing of intercourse and the regularity of a woman's menstrual cycle are extremely important in conception.

Now, let's talk about the whole "women over the age of 35" bit. This part of the definition of *my least favorite word* was recently added, and it bothers me. This "over the age of 35" focus has us as a society freaking out and completely focused on a lack of fertility. There are *many* women who get pregnant and carry to term after the age of 35. I say, let's focus on *those* women.

Our Western world, modern reproductive medical-minded society says the reason for the rise of "fertility challenges" is simple: since the 1970s the proportion of women in the United States having their first baby at or after age 30 has quadrupled.

QUADRUPLED. To the Western medical world, the fact that women are having children later in life (over the age of 35) explains why our population is suddenly having such a hard time getting pregnant. From my 10 years of clinical experience, I definitely don't believe age is our only issue; it may be an issue for some, but it's not the major issue at play here. Here's some outstanding research that was published in the magazine *The Atlantic* in June 2013 rebutting that age is our biggest deterrent to fertility:

> The widely cited statistic that one in three women ages 35 to 39 will not be pregnant after a year of trying, for instance, is based on an article published in 2004 in the journal *Human Reproduction*. Rarely mentioned is the source of the data: French birth records from 1670 to 1830. The chance of remaining childless—30 percent—was also calculated based on historical populations. In other words, millions of women are being told when to get pregnant based on statistics from a time before electricity, antibiotics, or fertility treatment. Most people assume these numbers are based on large, well-conducted studies of modern women, but they are not.

In fact, of the more recent studies on age and fertility, science shows that age isn't as big of a fertility issue as we have been told. In 2004, the journal *Obstetrics & Gynecology* found that with sex at least twice a week, 82% of 35- to-39-year-old women conceive within a year, compared with 86% of 27- to 34-year-olds. Another study in 2013 out of the journal *Fertility and Sterility* found that 78% of 35- to 40-year-old women who were having sex at their fertile times (more on the timing of sex in chapter 2) got pregnant within a year, compared with 84% of 20- to 34-year-olds.

I recommend you shift your focus. Let's look at the fertility-focused side of the equation: plenty of women in their 30's and 40's are getting pregnant. Look around you, there's a lot of conceiving going on. I'm sure we all know at least a few women who have gotten pregnant at 35, 38, 40, and 42. Age is not the major issue here. Truth is, the process of getting pregnant is so multidimensional that for one woman it might just be a matter of having more timely sex, for another it may be that she needs to change her diet, for another it may be she needs to work through her anger towards her mother (yes, I'm serious!), for another it could be her chronic exposure to hormone-disrupting toxins (also known as endocrine-disrupting chemicals) in her shampoo or makeup, for another it may be her husband's sperm (we will discuss sperm in chapter 2), for another it may be her autoimmune disease (discussed in chapter 3), and for yet another it may be all of the above. That's a lot of variables. I've seen them all play a part in a couple's or a woman's ability (or inability) to conceive. Most importantly, being focused on a lack of fertility is going to have a negative impact on your fertility. This is how I see it: focusing on the lack of fertility causes you stress and Western science has shown through innumerable research studies that stress causes hormonal disruptions and this in turn negatively affects your fertility. We need to shift the focus.

I want you to become fertility focused as there is a lot of fertility going on. Fact is, there is more fertility than there isn't, meaning more women get pregnant than don't. You can be one of those fertile women.

Fertility from a Traditional Oriental Medicine Perspective

Here's the way I view my fertility patients: not one patient is like any other. Just as we are all intricately different, our "fertility challenges" are also different. My resulting treatment plan from a Traditional Oriental Medicine (TOM) perspective and recommendations are completely different from one patient to the next. I could have three different women come in with the same Western medical diagnosis of "high FSH" (FSH = follicle stimulating hormone; more on that in the next chapter) and they will all be treated differently. That's the big distinction between Western and Eastern medicine. In TOM we diagnose based on individual patient presentations; we call it pattern discrimination. So, rather than just doing blood work, listening to a patient's symptoms, doing a urinalysis or an MRI, and diagnosing someone with a disorder, a practitioner of TOM will spend a couple of hours discussing with a patient his or her medical history, diet, and emotional state to come up with an individual pattern diagnosis.

When I spend time with my patients, I don't just talk to them about the obvious fertility topics such as menstrual cycles and ovulation, I talk about bowel movements and sleep and diet and energy levels, sex drives, lifestyle factors, environmental stressors, and their dominant emotional states. A TOM practitioner focuses on the root cause of illness, not just on symptoms. TOM takes into account every aspect of every person—body, mind, spirit—as there is so much more that goes into fertility than just physiology and how well your uterus and ovaries work.

One of the first questions I have had for every single fertility patient I have ever seen is: do you believe you are going to get pregnant? I'm happy to say that most often the answer is "yes." It's not usually a confident yes, it's a hesitant one that usually comes with tears. But it's a yes.

So let's take a moment and I want you to ask yourself, "Do I believe I am going to get pregnant?" Hear the answer. See the answer. Replace doubt with hope. And if the pregnant question is hard to answer, then how about, "Do I believe I am going to be a mother?"

In TOM we look at pregnancy and motherhood as something you prepare for, not something that should just spontaneously happen. In Eastern medicine we are all about prevention and preparation, unlike Western medicine where they need a problem to fix. In Eastern medicine, we believe that one needs to be aligned emotionally *and* physically for optimal health and optimal fertility to be present. By aligned, I mean health must be in check on every level: mental, emotional, nutritional, and physiological. Not to say that misaligned people don't get pregnant, they do. However, a pregnancy and a child that comes from alignment is much more healthful and balanced than one that does not. And, a child that is raised around alignment will be more aligned. It perpetuates itself.

Here's something to think about: between 30% and 40% of fertility cases are diagnosed as being "idiopathic," which means "of an unknown cause." These patients appear perfectly normal from a Western physiological perspective: they menstruate regularly, they ovulate when they should, their bloodwork looks perfect, their partners' sperm is great, yet for some reason they are not getting pregnant. However, when these "idiopathic" cases wind up in my clinic, I find many misalignments from a TOM perspective (and sometimes from a Western perspective as well), and most commonly they are of a mental–emotional nature. In TOM, the mental–emotional state of a patient is of utmost importance to her health and her ability to conceive. That's why I urge all of my patients to prepare for pregnancy, especially on the psychological front. That is also why I'm being so redundant about this whole believing in your body thing. It's a big deal. If you don't believe in your body and its fertility, it's going to be hard to get pregnant.

Preparing Your Child's Palace

TOM emphasizes the importance of *preparing your child's palace* prior to conception and pregnancy. So what does this mean exactly? In the Chinese language, the term uterus is called: *zi gong*. When translated to English this means, "the child's palace." The word *palace* is referring to your uterus. When we talk about your uterus, we are not just talking about an organ. Your uterus is an extension of you physically and mentally. Every organ in our body has both a physiological component *and* an emotional one. By physiological, I mean its role in our body's ability to function, such as its ability to sleep or digest food. By emotional, I mean that each organ's ability to function optimally is positively or negatively influenced by particular emotional states, such as anger, fear, joy, or contentment. Just as our health can be improved or impaired by how we physically take care of it, it can also be affected by how we emotionally manage our lives.

When it comes to the health of your uterus, your child's palace, we are talking about a precious place that from a physiological perspective houses and nurtures life, and from an emotional perspective is a manifestation of the amount of joy and courage you have (or don't). Your uterine health isn't just determined by your uterine lining or the regularity of your menstrual cycle; it involves how the food you eat, the amount of sleep you get, how happy you are, and the quality of the life you're living affects both the *emotional and physical* health of your uterus. Preparing your child's palace means getting your body, mind, and spirit aligned and open to pregnancy.

The Emotional Health of Your Child's Palace

Your child's palace is a very spiritual place and the health of it depends not just upon anatomy and physiology, diet, and lifestyle; it is also powerfully affected by the following two emotional factors:

1. The courage to believe in your body and its ability to procreate, and
2. Having joy and passion in your life.

Yes, joy and passion and the courage to have a resolute belief in your body are imperative to healthy conception and pregnancy.

When it comes to your child's palace, the emotional states that affect it have to do with two other organs, the heart and kidneys. The uterus is seen as being an extension of the heart and the kidneys, and therefore it is affected by the dominant emotional state of these two organs. Your child's palace is linked to the heart and kidneys via two direct vessels: one that connects the heart to the uterus and one that connects the kidneys to the uterus. These vessels are direct lines of communication between the heart and uterus and the kidneys and the uterus. It is through this connection that each of these organs has a strong influence on the health and vitality of your child's palace.

The heart's emotional component is positively influenced by joy and passion and is negatively affected by worry and anxiety. The kidneys are positively influenced by courage and confidence and negatively affected by fear and trauma. So when you have thoughts of passion and joy, you send the goodness of those thoughts into your child's palace. Alternatively, if you have fear and worry, you send those negative, burdensome emotions to your child's palace. What kind of palace would you want to live in, a passionate joyful one or a fearful worrisome one? The TOM viewpoint is that joy, passion, courage, and confidence bolster the uterus's function where worry, anxiety, fear, and trauma impair it.

Improve your fertility with:

- **Joy**
- **Passion**
- **Courage**
- **Confidence**

In the next chapter we will get into more of the anatomy and physiology of reproduction from both an Eastern and a Western standpoint, but for now we are solely focused on what we are feeling when we think about our child's palace.

Pause for a moment and really let what I just said sink in. *Think about it: what emotions or feelings do you feel when you think about your uterus, the palace that is meant to hold your child?*

Do you even think about this organ emotionally? Do you ever send your uterus love or positive thoughts?

Every time you have a negative thought or a fearful feeling about your ability to conceive, you are sending a message to your child's palace that says: I don't believe in you. This type of thinking can hurt your ability to get pregnant. The moment you decide to believe that you can't have children or that you will have trouble conceiving, you convince your body and your child's palace of the same message. That's why I can't stress enough that you believe in your body, focus on all the fertility around you, and remove *my least favorite word* from your vocabulary.

You have the ability to make an emotional choice and to free yourself of the worrisome burdens that you are carrying, and this choice will open your body up to receive, in all aspects of your life. I will offer you many tools on how to unburden your heart in chapter 7 (and get much more into our emotions); however, for now I want to talk about how emotions can affect the degree of health of your child's palace. Please note: from here on out your uterus will be known as your child's palace. Say it out loud, daily, write it on a stickie and place it on your bathroom mirror, or do both.

Bottom line: this palace is your new favorite place, so send it love every day and make it amazing and happy and gleaming with joy.

An excerpt from a recent patient e-mail:

I AM PREGNANT!
I am crying writing this. I could not thank you enough...the acupuncture, the nutrition, but most importantly just being so supportive and someone that I could really talk to. You helped me to stay calm, believe in my body again and be positive—three things that are usually very hard for me to do!!

Joy and Courage

Let's get a little more of a grasp on this emotional heart→uterus← kidneys connection so you can start making changes to improve your fertility.

First, the heart. The heart in TOM plays an extremely significant role when it comes to emotions: it rules our spirit. Our spirit is our inner radiance. Our spirit is said to be housed in the heart and it is what brings brightness to our life and is responsible for consciousness and mental abilities. Your spirit is wholeheartedly affected by how much joy you have in your life. If you are happy and positive and looking at life with gratitude and optimism, then your inner radiance is bright and your heart and your spirit are flourishing and flowing well. Healthy Qi (pronounced

---

The Heart Rules Our Spirit

It is our inner radiance.
It loves joy, gratitude, and positivity.
Our spirit suffers when we have anxiety, negativity, and sorrow.
Boost your spirit each day: upon waking, make a list of five things that bring you joy.

13

Chee—an imperative substance in our bodies that gives us life and allows us to function properly) to your child's palace.

On the other hand, your spirit is negatively affected by how much anxiety and sadness you have in your life. These two emotions, anxiety and sadness, when experienced over long periods of time, are said to sever the channel that flows from your heart to your uterus and this will hinder fertility. The antidote to anxiety and sadness severing this channel is joy. Joy is the key.

> *Qi is our life force.*
> *Qi is at the root of our health and vitality.*
> *Without Qi there is no life.*

Next, the kidneys. The kidneys house our essence. Essence is an extremely precious substance. In fact, in TOM, we consider essence the most important substance as it is the foundation of our health, longevity, and ability to procreate (we will talk about essence a great deal throughout this book, but for now understand that just as the heart houses our spirit, the kidneys house essence, and these two things are fundamental to our ability to get and stay pregnant). The positive emotion of the kidneys is courage. When we have courage and the will to have a resolute belief in our body and its ability to procreate, our kidneys are flowing strong-willed and powerful Qi and essence to the uterus.

> *Essence is our foundation of healthy, longevity, and fertility.*
> *Essence loves courage and confidence.*
> *Our essence suffers when we have fear and doubt.*
> *Support your essence by letting go of fear and having faith in your body.*

However, fear and doubt block our kidney energy. These emotions limit the kidneys' ability to nourish the child's palace. I'm not saying you don't have any courage, as I am sure that you do. Even with picking up this book you are taking a courageous step toward trying to improve your fertility. But I am saying that doubt is the sister to fear, and if you're doubting your body and its ability to have a child then you are, on some level, even if it's a minor one, affecting your kidney–uterus connection.

Another place fear comes from is past trauma. Whether it was a big life event like the death of a loved one or sexual abuse or a miscarriage or a divorce or going bankrupt, trauma like that can sever our kidney–uterus connection. This type of trauma deserves attention and a decision to work through it. We can't sequester these events and hope they will just go away. It doesn't work that way. Unexpressed or repressed emotions will eat at us, and traumatic ones that haven't been dealt with can really have an impact on our fertility (we will get into this in greater detail in chapter 7).

The emotions of sadness and anxiety hurt our spirit and our heart and this in turn can sever or block the heart's connection to the uterus and hinder fertility. Similarly, fear and doubt hurt our essence and our kidneys, and this can sever or block the kidney–uterus connection, with fertility being negatively affected. We say in TOM that in order for life to be created, the spirit and essence must meet and mingle in the uterus. We need the brightness of our spirit and the courage and will of our essence to create a fertile child's palace and a baby that can be nurtured in that palace.

Trauma

Traumatic events can happen in many areas over a lifetime and can leave us with emotional, physical, psychological, and sexual wounds. Traumatic events can leave us feeling numb and disconnected, frightened and fearful, anxious and overwhelmed. In both Western and Eastern medicine undealt-with trauma can have seriously negative effects on your health. If you feel as if you have had past traumas that you haven't yet recovered from, this could be affecting not only your health but your fertility. Seek professional help to unburden your body from this trauma. You deserve to let go of past traumas. You deserve to feel good.

Emotions in Action

I met Kristin when she was 39 and engaged to be married. She was in a great place, excited about life: she loved her job, she loved her man, and she couldn't wait to start a family. She came to my office for a back problem she developed from running. However, at our first visit she also mentioned she wanted to make sure she could get pregnant right away once she got married. Due to all her running, her periods were quite light and often when she was training hard for a race she would miss a period. As we worked together, she started running less and eating more healthy fats and animal protein. Her period got healthier and extremely regular and, on her honeymoon, she got pregnant. At about eight weeks into her pregnancy, she miscarried. It was a hard thing to take, as it always is, but she and her husband were eager to try again once they could. About four months later she got pregnant again. This time the pregnancy took, but at about 20 weeks we found that the fetus had a terminal chromosomal abnormality (which was "age-indiscriminate," meaning it was just as likely to happen to a 20-year-old woman as it was to a 40-year-old woman) and her doctors told Kristin she should terminate the pregnancy. It was crushing.

After two failed pregnancies, her demeanor began to shift. She lost her generally bubbly nature; she started having regular bouts of insomnia and anxiety over anything and everything. Her heart was burdened, her spirit was fractured, and her essence was traumatized. Until we restored her faith in her body and its ability to conceive she was not going to get pregnant again.

As time moved on, she went to fertility doctors, she did three IUIs (intrauterine inseminations) and two IVFs. None of them worked. She changed doctors. She got second and third opinions. Her doctors recommended doing a donor egg cycle (an IVF with someone else's egg). We kept up our treatments, and we would have deep conversations, but every time I tried to get her to tell me if she had faith in her body she would just sob. She admitted she didn't believe in her body any longer. She felt as if it had failed her. She was angry at her body and her uterus. She eventually took a break from all the fertility treatments.

One day at a business meeting, Kristin met a woman who was in her mid-40s and pregnant. They got to talking and they shared stories. Their stories were almost exactly the same. But, this woman was pregnant and Kristin was not. The woman told Kristin about how she had started meditating and visualizing herself pregnant with a healthy baby that she would deliver. This woman told Kristin how she "forgave" her body for letting her down in the past and became positive again in its ability to do what it had always longed to do: get pregnant with a healthy child. Soon after, Kristin told me about this woman's story. As she relayed to me all the details, she appeared the most hopeful and optimistic I had seen her in over a year. We talked more about the emotional connection to fertility and about how her emotions affect her child's palace and for the first time in a long time I felt she heard me. I saw her spirit light up again. The old Kristin was back. And, even though it took a few months, she got pregnant *naturally*. As I write this, Kristin is 42 and she is 6 months pregnant with a healthy baby girl. I don't know if your eyes are filled with tears, but I cry every time I tell the story. It's just so clear: our emotions truly, completely affect our ability to conceive.

Here's another story that you might relate to. Sosha had her first appointment with me three weeks prior to the beginning of her first IVF cycle. Ten months prior Sosha had gotten pregnant naturally, on her and her husband's first attempt at pregnancy. She miscarried at six weeks. Right after her miscarriage, she frantically contacted her gynecologist. As Sosha was only 29 at the time, her doctor told her that miscarriages are common (they are) and that she should just continue trying naturally. But at that point Sosha had already read too many of those online fertility forums and she was now convinced that she'd never get pregnant naturally. She was convinced she needed help from fertility doctors. She started doing IUI's with clomid; she did three cycles, they all failed. Then she pushed for IVF even though her husband was against it. When she came to me she anxiously explained how IVF was her only option, how nothing else was going to work for her. And she *needs* to get pregnant, *now*.

As we went through our initial intake I asked her if she and her husband still had a good sex life. She snickered and gave me this look like: are you serious? She admitted they hadn't had good sex since the miscarriage. She no longer enjoyed sex. She no longer had orgasms. Sex was just something they had to do to try to get pregnant. I then asked her if they used to have a good sex life. She started to cry and told me, "it was the best sex ever." A week later, due to some insurance delays Sosha was told she had to wait another month until she could begin IVF. Soon after, she came into my office and told me about the delay. As we talked, she asked me, "Do you think there's a shot I can get pregnant this month if we try naturally and do acupuncture every week?"

I said, "I only recommend trying this month if you are willing to have faith that it can work. Do you believe you can get pregnant naturally?"

She said, sarcastically, "I'll do whatever you tell me to do."

I said, "I want you to look in the mirror every morning and say into the mirror: 'I believe in my body and its ability to get pregnant.' And, one more thing, when you have sex you need to have an orgasm. However you can get yourself there, you need to. Period."

I saw her once a week through that menstrual cycle and at each visit, while I put acupuncture needles in her, we talked about her having faith in her body again, we talked about how to get the sexy intimacy back with her husband, we talked about her life and the things she was currently grateful for. That month, she wore sexy lingerie and got her mojo back. And guess what? She got pregnant naturally. She had a baby girl about six months ago. She never needed IVF. It wasn't her fertility that was broken, it was her heart. She had just lost faith in her body. Like so many women trying to get pregnant, she let fear, anxiety, and doubt take over.

> *Take a moment right now and repeat your new mantra:*
> I have the power to change MY health and improve
> MY fertility.

Later on in this book, we will dig deeper into the connection between your mental–emotional state and your fertility, but from the above stories, I hope you can see how, for many of us, very often fear and anxiety and sadness can cause fertility challenges. Before we move on to the next chapter, I want you to take a few moments and ponder the following two questions:

1. How much joy and passion do I have in my life?
2. How much do I believe in my body and its ability to procreate?

Hopefully, you are conscious of some joy and passion in your life. Hopefully you believe in your body at least a little bit. Either way, I want you to focus more on the joyful things in your life. I want you to reawaken your passions. I want you to believe in your body. The rest of this book will offer you a great amount of useful information that you can apply right now, but before we move forward, I want you to focus on experiencing joy, gratitude, and confidence daily. These emotions will bring you into an alignment that will help you conceive.

I'd like you to do these three things starting today:

1. Before going to bed each night, write down five things that brought you joy that day. It could be something simple like: I had an awesome healthy lunch; it was great to catch up with Jane—talking with her makes me happy; my workout today felt great; my relationship brings me such joy; or, I had a great hair day and that makes me happy.

2. Each morning, speak this simple affirmation to your child's palace: while lying down, put your hands over your lower abdomen and speak this affirmation either aloud or in your head:

    Dear Uterus, you are the palace of my child and I believe in you. I send you love and joy. You are a beautiful palace, brimming with fertility, and I fully believe in your ability to get pregnant.

3. And promise me, from here on out, *my least favorite word* will be forever removed from your vocabulary. If you really need to talk about it, use "fertility challenged" or "subfertile."

I need you to decide to embrace courage and hope and look for joyful things in your life each and every day. Without these conscious changes, getting pregnant is going to be more difficult than it needs to be. Reclaim your fertility. Believe in your body. Send love to your child's palace. That's enough emotional talk, *for now*. Turn the page and let's get into some anatomy and physiology.

2
Your Fertile Body: Understanding How It Works

In order for you to really begin rejuvenating your fertility and to ultimately get pregnant, first you need to believe in the power you have to change your health and your fertility, all the stuff we covered in chapter 1 (if you skipped that chapter, go back and reread it now.). Second, you need to understand how your womanly parts work. When we understand how a bodily system, like your reproductive system, optimally operates, we can then take that knowledge to figure out why your system isn't working optimally and find the best way to get it back on track. As well, when we appreciate the sophisticated details of what goes on inside our body we form a strong foundation in understanding how powerful our bodies are and how susceptible they are to minor changes, both in positive and negative directions. This chapter will go over the ins and outs of your reproductive system, your menstrual cycle, how conception occurs from both a Western and Eastern medical perspective, and will help you understand your anatomy and physiology so that you have the knowledge and the power to improve your fertility and get pregnant.

Your Optimal Menstrual Cycle

When I first meet a fertility client, we talk about how her menstrual cycle is functioning. There are three key phases to the menstrual cycle, and how those phases function (or dysfunction) tells me a lot about how her reproductive system is working. I look for these cues to determine the state of her fertile body. Below is how an optimal menstrual cycle presents in a female of reproductive age:

1. A regular menstrual cycle comes every 28 to 35 days. The flow should be bright red blood and come and go in a tapered fashion: the first one to two days are the heaviest (about six to eight teaspoons of blood per day or six to eight regular tampons/pads or three to four super tampons/pads) and the flow tapers off gently over the next two to three days (about two to four teaspoons of blood per day or two to four regular tampons/pads). There should be minimal clotting with slight breast tenderness and very little cramping.

2. Efficient ovulation occurs between cycle days 14 to 21, with cycle day one being the first day of your menstrual flow. This means that day one of your cycle is the first day you bleed, so counting from there ovulation should occur somewhere between cycle day 14 to 21. The day of ovulation varies depending on the average cycle length of a menstrual cycle. Ovulation should come at the mid-point of your menstrual cycle, so if you typically have a 30-day cycle (again with day one being the first day you bleed), ovulation should occur on or around cycle day 15. Ovulation should come with a few days of clear, egg white cervical mucus and an increased sex drive. Some women feel a slight twinge or heaviness in their ovaries at this time, and although not every woman feels this, feeling this is considered normal. As well, some women will feel slight breast tenderness, and this is also considered normal. If you are tracking your basal body temperature (BBT) (see page 25), this is the time of the month when your basal temperature should rise at least 0.4 of a degree.

3. The luteal phase is a 12 to 14 day phase starting after ovulation that lasts until the next menstrual cycle begins. It should be free of any major premenstrual symptoms such as extreme breast

tenderness, heavy cramping, spotting, extreme mood swings, and fatigue. Normal symptoms occurring at the tail end of this phase (i.e., a few days before your period is due) are mild lower back and/or lower abdomen cramping, slight breast tenderness, slight mood sensitivity, and subtle food cravings.

If a client's menstrual cycle is functioning well, it indicates that her hormones are working as they should and, generally, her reproductive system is functioning optimally. If your period is not functioning optimally right now, don't fret, as this book will help you achieve a more fertile body even if yours is a touch out of balance at the moment. In chapter 4 I give specific recommendations about how to balance each phase of the menstrual cycle. Before we get to all of that, however, it is important to note that there is a lot more that goes into pregnancy and conception than just your menstrual cycle. There is an extremely intricate hormonal cascade at work in your body that is constantly working to not only regulate your menstrual cycle but also to prepare you for conception and pregnancy.

The Basis of Your Fertile Body

Truly, the human body is a miraculous place, and you have the power to make your body a miraculously fertile place. As I mentioned in the last chapter, having a resolute belief in the wondrousness of your beautiful fertile body is the first and most important step in rejuvenating your fertility. So, as you read on, take all the information on the pages that follow, digest it, and own the fact that you have an amazing fertile body.

From a Western medical perspective, the basis of your fertile body comes down to something called the hypothalamus–pituitary–ovarian axis (HPO axis). This HPO axis is an intricate interaction between two parts of your brain (the hypothalamus and the pituitary gland), your precious ovaries (yes, they are *very* precious as they contain the egg that will one day become your baby), and the palace of your child: your uterus.

It all starts in the brain, at your hypothalamus, which is located at the base of your brain. The hypothalamus releases a hormone called gonadotropin-releasing hormone (GnRH). This hormone travels to another area of the brain, the pituitary gland, and tells it to release two fundamental fertile body hormones: follicle-stimulating hormone (FSH) and luteinizing hormone (LH). These two hormones are released into the bloodstream in a specific and timely fashion (first FSH is released and then, later in the menstrual cycle, LH is released) and travel down to your ovaries. FSH tells your ovaries to start recruiting and maturing follicles from your ovarian reserve. Follicles are basically little sacs, each containing an egg that can one day get fertilized by sperm and become a baby.

As FSH stimulates the ovaries to develop healthy and mature follicles, these same follicles start secreting estrogen, which also helps them mature and grow bigger. Estrogen, being released by the follicles, also causes your uterine lining to thicken so that there is a healthy blood supply in your uterus to nourish an embryo if one implants. As estrogen levels increase with increasing size of mature follicles in your ovaries, it sends a message back to the hypothalamus to stop releasing GnRH. This message from increased estrogen levels to the hypothalamus causes the pituitary gland to *stop* releasing FSH and to *start* releasing LH. This release of LH causes the most mature follicle in your ovary to burst open and ovulate out an egg. For those of you who have used ovulation predictor kits to determine when you are ovulating, the hormone those kits detect is LH.

Are you scienced out yet? I know this may seem like information that only a doctor needs to know; however, I really want you to take back the power of your fertility and this information will arm you with that power. Just like anything else, when you understand how it works, figuring out how to fix it is that much easier.

After ovulation has occurred, the follicular sac that once encapsulated your egg starts producing the hormone progesterone. This progesterone is imperative to the phase of your menstrual cycle after ovulation, the luteal phase, which is a 12 to 14 day waiting period that starts after ovulation and continues until the menstrual cycle begins again. Progesterone secretion during the luteal phase is extremely important as it maintains and holds in place your healthy uterine lining; increases the internal temperature of your body and uterus so that it can hold a pregnancy if conception occurs; and tells your pituitary gland to stop releasing LH. If conception happens, progesterone will continue to be secreted to maintain the pregnancy. If conception doesn't happen, progesterone levels drop off, your uterus sheds its uterine lining, you get your period, and the entire cycle begins anew. Don't worry if this is all not forming a clear picture for you; I have a diagram below to map it all out for you.

To recap:

- The hypothalamus releases GnRH, which tells the pituitary gland to first release FSH.
- FSH causes the ovaries to start recruiting and growing mature follicles.
- Maturing follicles release estrogen.
- Estrogen thickens the uterine lining and also tells the pituitary gland to stop producing FSH and start producing LH.
- LH causes ovulation to occur.
- Ovulation is the rupturing of the follicular sac that contains an egg.
- The follicular sac produces progesterone.
- Progesterone maintains the uterine lining and warms up the body to prepare for pregnancy.
- Pregnancy either happens and progesterone levels are maintained or pregnancy doesn't happen (this month!) and progesterone levels drop off, the uterus sheds its lining, and the entire cycle begins again.

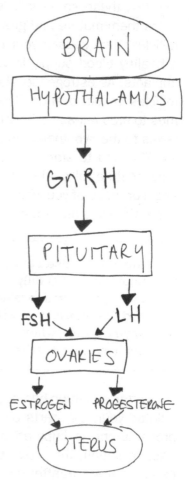

BBT Charting

Some women find it useful to track and chart their BBT (basal body temperature), which is the temperature of your body at rest, to determine when they ovulate as well as the regularity of the phases of their menstrual cycle. The key with taking your BBT is that you must take it daily upon waking, before getting out of bed, and it is most accurate when taken after four to five hours of uninterrupted sleep.

For some of my clients, this daily BBT tracking is helpful, but for other women it can be very stressful. So I tell women to do this BBT charting only if they feel good about doing it, as the added stress isn't the best for fertility.

What's interesting, though, is to see how a normal BBT chart should look and how it correlates with the hormonal cascade that is responsible for your menstrual cycle. Here's what a typical BBT chart should look like (based on a 28-day menstrual cycle). Notice how your BBT shifts in accordance with the release of the hormones in your body:

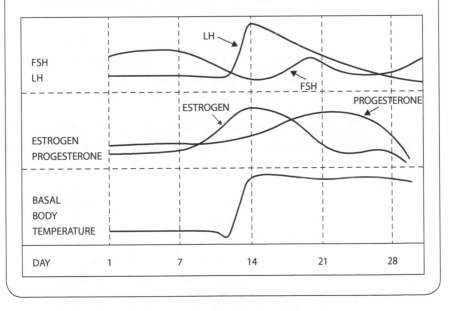

And all of this is happening while you're just going through your day. I don't know about you, but I find this whole process absolutely amazing. In chapter 10, we will get into specific Western-diagnosed "fertility challenges" your body may be going through. But let's briefly cover some of the challenges that are related to the HPO axis and offer you some quick tips to help jump-start an optimal menstrual cycle. The three biggest fertility issues that come from an out-of-whack HPO axis are imbalances in the following hormones:

- FSH

  ○ FSH is tested in cycle day two or three (with cycle day one being the first day of bleeding), and your doctor wants to see an FSH at or less than 10 mIU/mL. An FSH below 10 indicates good ovarian reserve; anything higher than 10 is a sign of diminishing ovarian reserve.

  ○ FSH is secreted by the pituitary gland and tells the ovaries to start recruiting and maturing follicles. When an FSH is already high (above 10) on cycle day two or three it means that the ovaries are asking the brain for more FSH because it is running low on follicles.

  ○ Important to know: your FSH number is not static, meaning it will vary from month to month.

> Don't get attached to your FSH number. Women with "high FSH" get pregnant naturally all the time.

  ○ High FSH levels suggest a diminished ovarian reserve but they do not mean you will not be able to get pregnant naturally. In fact, many women with a poor ovarian reserve do get pregnant naturally.

  ○ FSH can be altered by high levels of estrogen and less commonly by pituitary tumors and adrenal hyperplasia.

  ○ Two other tests: AMH (anti-mulleurian hormone) and the antral follicle count are more accurate determinants of ovarian reserve in comparison to FSH levels. AMH is a hormone secreted by "good quality" follicles and tends to decrease with age; the antral follicle count is done via ultrasound where your doctor will look at your ovaries and see how many "antral" follicles are growing.

- The best thing to do naturally to lower FSH is to avoid all environmental estrogens pesticides, plastics, sulfates and parabens in your body and beauty products, and follow the *Yes, You Can Get Pregnant* diet outlined in chapter 5.
- My favorite supplements to support lowering FSH naturally are spirulina, royal jelly, and wheat grass (there will be more on supplements in chapter 5).

- Estrogen
  - Estrogen, in the form of estradiol or E2 (all three terms are used interchangeably), is usually tested on cycle day two or three along with FSH. Ideally, estrogen levels should be between 25 and 75 pg/mL at this point in your cycle (the lower the better).
  - Estrogen is secreted by growing follicles in your ovaries and is an indicator of how well these follicles are growing.
  - If estrogen is high there may be a cyst that is secreting estrogen (and preventing a timely ovulation) or it may be a sign of hyper-thyroidism (to be discussed more in chapter 10). Lastly, and what I see as most common, high estrogen levels are a result of estrogen dominance, which is abundant in our society at the moment due to all of the environmental estrogens affecting our hormone levels.
  - If estrogen is too low it can mean that there are not very many maturing follicles in your ovaries, or in the case of polycystic ovarian syndrome (PCOS) there are several follicles trying to develop but they never reach a mature stage so estrogen levels remain low. As well, low estrogen levels can indicate a tendency toward a thin uterine lining, which could prevent implantation of an embryo. In my clinic, we typically see low levels of estrogen in women with eating disorders (or a recent history of one), women who are extreme exercisers, and women who are underweight.
  - The best thing to do to keep a balanced estrogen level is to not overexercise, to maintain a healthy weight, to follow the *Yes, You Can Get Pregnant* diet, and to avoid environmental estrogens (more on these in chapter 6). This is true for both

low and high estrogen levels as these changes will bring about balance to your hormonal system and estrogen will regulate itself.

  ○ My favorite supplements to balance estrogen levels are cod liver oil, spirulina, and wheat grass (more on these in chapter 5).

- Progesterone

  ○ As we discussed above, progesterone is secreted by what remains of the ruptured follicle (after ovulation has occurred and the egg is released). So, up until ovulation, progesterone levels remain quite low. Progesterone is typically tested around cycle day 20 (or approximately seven days postovulation) and should be around 15 to 20 ng/mL.

  ○ Following ovulation, this increase in progesterone helps further build the uterine lining to help prepare the uterus (your child's palace) for implantation, and it also causes a warming of the body (which is detectable when you are doing your BBT).

  ○ Progesterone levels usually start to elevate when an egg is released from the ovary, rise for several days, and then either continue to rise with early pregnancy or fall to initiate menstruation.

  ○ Progesterone plays two important roles in early stage pregnancy: (1) It relaxes the uterus and decreases the chances of contraction in the uterine muscles, and (2) it briefly inhibits your body's immune system so that the pregnancy is accepted by your body.

  ○ If progesterone levels do not rise and fall on a monthly basis, a woman may not be ovulating or having menstrual periods.

  ○ If progesterone levels are high it could indicate ovarian cysts or a problem with your adrenal glands.

  ○ If progesterone levels are low following ovulation this could indicate what is called a luteal phase defect (LPD). The luteal phase is that part of your menstrual cycle that begins after ovulation and lasts until your menstruation (or pregnancy) begins. When there is an LPD this means that the body is either not producing enough progesterone or the lining of your uterus doesn't respond to the progesterone in your body.

LPD can be a result of eating disorders, hypothyroidism, PCOS, endometriosis, excessive exercise, and obesity.

o The best way to treat a progesterone imbalance is to not over-exercise, to maintain a healthy weight, to follow the *Yes, You Can Get Pregnant* diet and, in particular, to focus on eating foods that are cooked (to support the warmer temperature of your body during this phase) and rich in a nutrient called beta-carotene. These foods tend to be yellow or orange in color, such as sweet potatoes, yams, and carrots.

o My favorite supplements to balance a progesterone issue are cod liver oil (more on this in chapter 5) and vitex (aka vitex agnus-castus, or chasteberry). Vitex is an herb that has been shown in studies to lengthen a short luteal phase, increase progesterone levels, and help prevent miscarriages. If you have a progesterone imbalance, I recommend 800 mg/d in capsule form. My favorite brand is Pure Encapsulation. However, as with any supplement, discuss first with your doctor before taking.

Now that we have a more detailed understanding of the HPO axis and how the specific hormones involved in your menstrual cycle affect your reproductive system, you have more power in managing your fertility and your ability to conceive. Next, let's discuss the phenomenal process of conception.

Your Fertile Body's Getting Some Action

There are many moving parts that need to come together for conception to occur. But don't let that worry you. Just look around and notice every single person you see, and realize that they were conceived. Yes, conception is a miracle, but it happens all the time and your fertile body is ready to conceive. Believe it. Remember: it is your job to have a resolute belief in your body and its ability to conceive.

Using that strong belief in your body and the knowledge that you have the power to improve your health and fertility as the jumping-off point, let's talk about how your body is going to go about conceiving. Just as understanding the intricacies of the HPO axis is

*Take a moment right now and say to yourself
I have faith in my body's ability to conceive.
I have the power to change MY health and
improve MY fertility*

going to assist you in getting pregnant, getting comfortable with how conception occurs will also empower your fertility rejuvenation. The more you know about your reproductive system and how it works, the more power you have over your fertility.

Did you know that the process of conception begins anywhere from one to five days before ovulation even occurs? The events that occur leading up to ovulation are crucial. Here they are:

1. Sperm, about a teaspoonful, which contains two to three million spermatozoa, enters the vaginal canal, survives the swim from the vagina through the cervix, enters the uterus, and finds its way to the fallopian tubes. The time it takes for sperm to swim from the vagina into the uterus can be less than an hour, however, there are many steps that the sperm needs to go through to be able to fertilize an egg—these steps can take 10 to 24 hours.
2. The cervix must be open (it naturally opens wider at the time of ovulation) and your fallopian tubes clear for sperm to get to where it needs to be to meet the egg.
3. Sperm needs to be in the fallopian tubes hanging out, ready and waiting, prior to ovulation, as the egg, once ovulated, moves out of the follicular sac and through the fallopian tubes. If the egg is not fertilized it only lives for 12 to 24 hours. Sperm can live for up to five days in the uterus and fallopian tubes.

So the key is to get that healthy, super-swimming sperm up to the fallopian tubes *prior* to ovulation. It is typically in the fallopian tubes where egg and sperm meet. Then one spermatazoa needs to burrow through the outermost layers of the egg to fertilize it. Once this occurs, the now fertilized egg, or embryo, needs to travel down the fallopian tube into the uterus. This traveling can take

FEMALE REPRODUCTIVE SYSTEM

anywhere from three to seven days (an ectopic pregnancy is when the embryo gets stuck in the fallopian tube and tries to grow there rather than in the uterus). Once in the uterus the embryo now has to find a place to implant itself into the thick and blood-rich uterine lining. Then, in order for the embryo to continue to grow, the hormone progesterone must maintain the thick uterine lining.

Timing Tip

Sperm needs to be in the fallopian tubes, or at least on its journey up to the uterus, prior to ovulation. This means having sex *before* ovulation is key. I typically recommend patients start having sex about four days prior to ovulation and then every 24 to 36 hours.

For example: if you ovulate at cycle day 14, then you need to start trying on cycle day 9 and have sex every 24 to 36 hours until cycle day 15.

That's a lot of steps. But remember, conception happens *all the time.* Just look around you—all of the people you see were conceived. Believe that you, too, will conceive soon.

Next, an important topic that often gets overlooked when a couple is trying to conceive: orgasms.

Orgasms and Conception

I know, I know. The last thing you need to deal with when you're busy trying to get pregnant is feeling *pressure* to orgasm as well during sex. Of course, your partner must orgasm, but must you?

Well, some research indicates that the vaginal and uterine contractions that occur during a woman's orgasm help move sperm faster up through the cervix, into the uterus, and fallopian tubes. In fact, one study published by the journal *Archives of Sexual Behavior* measured the amount of semen "flowback" (how much semen leaked out after sex), and found that when female orgasm occurred a minute or less before male ejaculation, sperm retention was greater. They also found that this retention was higher even when the woman had an orgasm up to 45 minutes after male ejaculation. The theory here is that the more sperm you retain the better the odds of conception.

In Traditional Oriental Medicine (TOM) theory, we also believe female orgasm is extremely important for conception, as it brings the female joy (and, from the previous chapter, you know how important joy is in this whole process).

I don't want to pressure you, but I do want you to really try and enjoy sex, and even if you don't orgasm during sex, take the time to orgasm after sex. Let's be honest, orgasms feel great and you deserve to have passion with your partner and feel great during sex. And if you recall the story about Sosha from the last chapter, getting back to enjoying sex and having an orgasm absolutely helped her conceive.

There's one last thing we need to discuss: sperm. It plays a crucial role in conception.

Your Man, His Sperm, and Getting Preggers

Recent statistics show that about 30% of our population's fertility issues are male factor related. According to Western medicine, male factor issues are due to one of the following (or some, or all): low sperm count, poor sperm morphology (size and shape of sperm), or poor motility (sperm's ability to swim).

Spermatogenesis (the creation of sperm) depends upon the male version of the HPO axis (the hormonal cascade I described in detail to you earlier), just as the female menstrual cycle does; however, when it comes to men the hypothalamus and the pituitary gland release hormones that have an effect on the testicles (the male reproductive system) rather than the ovaries and uterus. The same hormones from the hypothalamus (GnRH) and the pituitary gland (FSH and LH) act on certain areas of the testicles to help men produce sperm. Similar to the female menstrual cycle and how FSH causes the follicles to mature and in turn begin secreting estrogen, in the male it is LH that acts on the testicles to cause them to secrete testosterone.

During the production of sperm in the testicles, there are quite a few things that can go wrong. However, because men typically create several million sperm at a time, poor sperm quality is not as critical a problem as say poor egg quality is (since a woman's egg quantity is continuously diminishing). If you have been trying to conceive for nearly 12 months and you haven't gotten pregnant, it's a good idea to get your man's sperm checked out.

Again, the things that can go wrong with sperm are threefold:

1. Low count
2. Poor shape (poor morphology)
3. Bad swimmers (poor motility)

Here are some factors you should be aware of that can affect the count, morphology, and motility of your man's sperm:

- Varicoceles: An abnormally enlarged and twisted (varicose) vein in the spermatic cord that connects to the testicle. These are found in about 15% of all men and in about 40% of infertile men. Varicoceles can raise testicular temperature, which may affect sperm production, movement, and shape.
- Infections: Repeated infections from sexually transmitted diseases such as chlamydia and gonorrhea or from viruses such as the mumps, human papilloma virus, or infections in the urinary tract or

genitals such as prostatitis (inflammation in the prostate gland), orchitis (in the testicle), semino-vesculitis (in the glands that produce semen), or urethritis (in the urethra) can affect sperm quality.

- Stress: Any major physical or mental stress can temporarily reduce sperm count.
- Testicular overheating: From high fevers, laptop use, saunas, and hot tubs, may temporarily lower sperm count.
- Substance abuse: Cocaine, marijuana, heavy alcohol consumption, and anabolic steroid use can temporarily reduce the quantity, quality, and motility of sperm.
- Smoking: Cigarette smoking may affect sperm quality.
- Obesity: Can impair hormonal levels and adversely affect fertility.
- Bicycling: Can affect erectile function as pressure from the bike seat may damage blood vessels and nerves that are responsible for erections.
- Toxic environmental chemicals such as herbicides, pesticides, and hormone-disrupting chemicals such as bisphenol A: May reduce sperm count by either affecting testicular function or altering hormone systems.
- Medical conditions: For example, a traumatic injury or major surgery (anywhere in the body), diabetes, HIV, thyroid disease, Cushing syndrome, heart attack, liver or kidney failure, and chronic anemia. Also some medications used to treat such conditions can affect sperm quality.
- Immunological problems: A man may have antisperm antibodies (immune or protective proteins) that attack and destroy his own sperm.

A handout to help you identify any sperm problems your man may have and more information on improving your man's sperm count and quality are available on my website, www.YesICanGetPregnant.com.

If you suspect a problem, get his sperm checked and be sure you have him follow the same dietary and supplement and lifestyle recommendations I will make for you throughout this book. Men have hormones, too, and the work we are going to do to balance your hormones, if incorporated into his life, will balance his hormones, too.

Now that we've covered the reproductive system, menstrual cycle, conception, and sperm from a Western medical perspective, next I want to discuss with you the reproductive system and conception from a TOM viewpoint.

The TOM Fertility Dance

The 5000-year-old medicine of TOM looks at fertility and conception a little more romantically than its Western counterpart. Fertility and conception are seen as a beautiful dance between three vital substances: Qi, blood, and essence. These three vital substances mingle together to create a life that will be housed in your child's palace. There is abundant essence, Qi, and blood flowing through your body, nourishing healthy, growing follicles that will ovulate mature eggs that dance and mate with sperm, and together they will nestle into a blood-rich vitalizing child's palace and create life. When all three vital substances are abundant and working in connection with one another, our health and fertility thrive and we should be able to conceive easily.

Essence, blood, and Qi are considered vital because without them life cannot exist; these substances are the basis for life. Essence and blood must mix to create Qi, which is life. These three vital substances are all we need and they are interdependent of one another. We have tenets in TOM that state: Essence is the root of Qi and blood; blood is the mother of Qi; Qi is the commander of blood. And what all this means is that they are all intertwined. Just like the ovaries could not function without the hypothalamus telling the pituitary gland to secrete certain hormones and the pituitary gland is not regulated without feedback from the estrogen-producing follicles from the ovaries, essence cannot exist without Qi and blood, nor can Qi and blood exist without essence.

It's simple, really: there are three vital substances—essence, Qi, and blood. When these three substances are abundant, and you live the right way, your health and fertility flourish. Period.

> *Remember your mantra, repeat it now:*
> I have the power to change MY health and improve
> MY fertility.

The power to improve your health and your fertility lies in all three of these vital substances, and most importantly in your essence. Essence is the foundation of our health, longevity, and ability to procreate. The foundation of your fertility is anchored primarily in your essence and secondarily in your blood and Qi. Since essence is of utmost importance with regard to fertility and conception, let's discuss it first.

> **The three vital substances imperative to your fertility are:**
>
> Essence
> Qi
> Blood

Essence

Essence is stored in the kidneys as an energetic reserve and is considered one of the most vital substances of the human body. It is at the root of menstrual regularity, ovarian reserve, ovulation, and the thick blood-rich uterine lining. Essence is the basis of life and as essence declines so does our health and our vitality. It's like the fire under a cauldron: without essence there is no fire to sustain life, nor fertility; without essence our body and its organs grow cold and wither away like a plant without sunlight. From a TOM perspective, our whole purpose is to preserve and consolidate our essence.

> Essence is the basis of life.

There are two types of essence, prenatal and postnatal:

- Prenatal essence is before-birth essence; it is the foundation from which we are created. This not only includes what the Western medical world would call our genetics, but also the embryonic environment in which we developed. So if mom and dad were super healthy and happy when they conceived you, and your mother took care of her health while she was pregnant with you, chances are you have a good reserve of prenatal essence. Alternatively, if your parents were living a not-so-healthy lifestyle, that, unfortunately, left you with less-than-ideal prenatal essence. Prenatal essence is completely out of our control. It is what it is.
- Postnatal essence is after-you've-been-born essence. This is the key to improving fertility. This is the goods. This type of essence is the health and longevity that we can create by eating and living as naturally as possible. This type of essence will affect the quality of your eggs (and the quality of your man's sperm). This is the stuff you can build all on your own. This is amazing news as the ball is in your court. Postnatal essence is critical and can override a potentially negative embryonic environment or a bad dose of prenatal essence and have a positive effect on our genetic predispositions (and I will show you how in great detail throughout this book).

Over the last decade there has been a significant amount of research going on into what Western medical science calls epigenetics, the study of how environmental factors influence how we age and how our genes react to our lifestyle. In TOM this is the same thing as postnatal essence. We will go into this more later, but for now I want you to realize that there is science behind this fact: the way you live your life, from the foods you eat, to how much you sleep, to how stressful your life is directly affects your postnatal essence and your fertility. I'm here to help you build up that postnatal essence so you can get and stay pregnant.

Bottom line: the more of this postnatal essence you can build up, the healthier and more fertile you will be (and the more health and fertility you will pass on to your child).

In addition to essence, the other two vital substances that are imperative to optimal fertility are blood and Qi.

Environmental Toxins and Our Fertility

"The scientific evidence over the last 15 years shows that exposure to toxic environmental agents before conception and during pregnancy can have significant and long-lasting effects on reproductive health. 'For example, pesticide exposure in men is associated with poor semen quality, sterility, and prostate cancer,' said Linda C. Giudice, MD, PhD, president of the American Society of Reproductive Medicine. 'We also know that exposure to pesticides may interfere with puberty, menstruation and ovulation, fertility, and menopause in women.'"

Blood, Qi, and Creating Life

Both blood and Qi have a close relationship with essence, and all three of these vital substances interact with one another and are interdependent on one another. Essence is at the root of Qi and blood, and both Qi and blood help build essence. They all work synergistically to create life. And, we need all three to be abundant for optimal fertility.

In TOM, blood is considered the most important liquid substance: it nourishes tissues and organs and its circulation is imperative for our bodies to function and is fundamental for hormonal balance and optimal fertility. Just as with essence, without blood life does not exist. Blood is created from two sources:

1. The food we eat.
2. Our essence.

We need to eat nutrient dense, healthy, wholesome foods that are close to nature to create blood. And at the same time, if we don't have a good reserve of essence, our body cannot create blood, either.

The second substance that is imperative to optimal fertility in TOM is Qi. Qi, usually translated as "vital energy," is the energy that underlies everything in the universe. Qi is our life force. Qi is at the root of our health and vitality. Without Qi there is no life.

The Qi inside our bodies comes from three sources:

1. The air we breathe*
2. The food we eat
3. Our essence

Here is the essential equation you need to know:

Abundant Essence + Blood + Qi → Abundant Fertility

Without all three of these substances—essence, blood, and Qi—we cannot create a healthy quality egg and we definitely cannot conceive a child nor carry a pregnancy to term. The power for you lies in the fact that you can build all of these three substances together. You do this by living a balanced life that is in touch with nature, eating a nutrient-dense diet filled with organic foods, breathing clean, expansive, nontoxic air, learning to manage your stress levels, and finding joy and passion in your daily life.

> I first met Joanna three years after she had undergone treatment for a rare disease in her left kidney. Even though her disease wasn't cancerous, the medical treatment her doctors used to treat her illness required the use of chemotherapy drugs (drugs used to treat cancer). Thankfully, the treatment worked and she recovered from her illness. Now, she wanted to get pregnant. But first we had to regulate her menstrual cycle because after she underwent the medical treatment for her kidney, her periods were extremely irregular and she didn't seem to be ovulating.

(continued)

---

* When I say, the air we breathe, I not only mean that the quality of the air you are breathing should be fresh, clean, and nontoxic, but in addition, the body and beauty products you are putting on your skin also need to be nontoxic. The skin is our body's largest organ and it literally breathes in all of the products you put on it.

(continued)

Prior to coming to my office, Joanna had met with a reproductive doctor to discuss her chances of getting pregnant naturally. The doctor did some blood work and found that Joanna's FSH was 88 mlU/mL (if you recall, ideal FSH levels are below 10). He told her that based on her high FSH, she was in perimenopause and that she was not a candidate for IVF nor did he think she would ever get pregnant naturally. Rather, he recommended that she go straight to a donor egg IVF cycle (meaning she should use a donor's egg as he didn't think her eggs were good based on her FSH level). Joanna was unaccepting of his advice and began to do her own research. She read in many places that acupuncture and TOM could help naturally lower her FSH and that's how she wound up in my office.

After doing my complete intake with Joanna, I diagnosed her with severe kidney essence deficiency (essence deficiency will lead to both Qi and blood deficiency as all three of these vital substances are interdependent on one another). In TOM, chemotherapy drugs, although life saving for many (Joanna included), are seen as being not only extremely toxic but also extremely detrimental to our essence, Qi, and blood. The way these drugs work is to kill off cells that are growing abnormally, but these medications also kill off our essence, Qi, and blood.

I immediately put Joanna on my *Yes, You Can Get Pregnant* diet, gave her Chinese herbs and supplements to take daily, and made her drink one to two cups per day of homemade bone broth (one of the most essence-building foods possible). As we worked on building her essence, a lot of Joanna's "perimenopausal" symptoms shifted: she had fewer night sweats, her hair stopped thinning, she had less vaginal dryness, and her periods came more regularly and with a healthier blood flow. After three months of regular acupuncture, dietary changes, Chinese herbs, supplements, and daily bone broth Joanna felt empowered and healthy and her FSH came down from

(continued)

(continued)

88 mlU/mL to 18 mlU/mL. It was amazing. And, although Joanna still needed to do IVF to get pregnant, she was able to use her own eggs. The work she and I did together restored her essence, Qi, and blood and rejuvenated her fertility. As I write this, Joanna is seven months pregnant and she has two embryos on ice.

In the pages that follow, you are going to get so much information on how to build up your postnatal essence, create healthy blood, and have abundant healthy Qi flowing through your body that your fertility challenges will become a thing of the past.

Let's take a moment and repeat your mantra
I have the power to change MY health and improve MY fertility.

Yes, you do! Turn the page and get a deeper understanding of the powerful role you play in rejuvenating your fertility.

3

How You Live Your Life Directly Affects Your Ability to Get Pregnant

Your fertility is not either working or broken, on or off; it is resilient and changeable. Yes, your fertility is changeable. You can improve your fertility. One thing you need to know: how you live your life emotionally, nutritionally, and physically affects your fertility. Just as you can influence your emotions, take charge over what you eat, and improve your fitness level, so too can you have control over your fertility.

Take a moment right now and repeat your new mantra:
I have the power to change MY health and improve
MY fertility.

Even if you have been told by your doctors that you are "fertility challenged" this does not mean you cannot still become pregnant. Furthermore, as I've seen with many of my patients, it's more likely that you never were lacking fertility; you probably just needed what I call: fertility rejuvenation. Fertility rejuvenation is all about restoring, revitalizing, and amplifying your fertility. It is about you taking back the power and taking control of your health and your fertility through dietary, lifestyle, and emotional modifications.

As we discussed earlier, the first step to rejuvenating your fertility is believing in your body and its ability to be fertile again. In this book, I am going to show you the *Yes, You Can Get Pregnant* way and give you solid, applicable advice that you can start living right now to help you get more fertile. Your job is to execute and apply the tools I give you to completely rejuvenate your fertility. But, remember, first you must *believe* you have the power to rejuvenate your fertility. I believe you do. I believe you have the capability to take back the power and become more fertile. If you keep in mind that your fertility is changeable, then you need to understand that the root of that ability is the fact that the way you live your life emotionally, nutritionally, and physically affects your health and your fertility. Your body is an amazing machine, and when exposed to optimal circumstances and pristine conditions it will thrive. Your body can heal miraculously, it can reverse an aging process, it can recover from major traumas, and rest assured, it can become more fertile.

There is an entire branch of science devoted to the idea that the way one lives one's life from an emotional, nutritional, and physical perspective can improve, or degrade, not just overall health, but fertility. This branch of science is called epigenetics. Epigenetics is the study of the how certain environmental factors (e.g., stress, diet, and environmental toxins) influence a set of chemical reactions that switch parts of a person's genome (the genetic material that makes you who you are) off and on at strategic times and locations, which together orchestrate the development and maintenance of an organism. Said another way, environmental factors such as stress, diet, behavior, and toxins activate chemical switches in your body that regulate whether certain genes get turned on or off, and this in turn affects your health status. From both a Western science–based and an Eastern philosophy–based perspective, there are things that you can do in your day-to-day life that positively affect your epigenetics, and there are things you do that can negatively affect your epigenetics. Again, your overall genetic makeup isn't changing, but how your genes work (or don't work) changes based on how you live your life.

> **Endocrine-Disrupting Chemicals (EDCs):** Chemicals in our environment that negatively affect how our hormones work and ultimately lead to reproductive disorders.

In 2010, *Frontiers in Endocrinology* published a paper entitled, "Epigenetic Effects of Endocrine-Disrupting Chemicals on Female Reproduction: An Ovarian Perspective." This study looked at environmental toxins such as pesticides in our foods, plastics, chemicals in our beauty products, and phytoestrogens (plant-based estrogenic compounds found in foods like soy) and how they affected our hormonal system, hence the term endocrine-disrupting chemicals (EDCs). Here are two big pieces of information that the researchers concluded from their study:

1. The overall fertility rate of women aged 15 to 44 years in the United States—measured by way of birth rates—dropped 44% between 1960 and 2002. Lifestyle choices have almost certainly been been a major contributor of this decline.
2. The "impaired fecundity rate" (i.e., the impaired ability to reproduce) increased from 11% to 15% between 1982 and 2002. Furthermore, the incidence of female reproductive disorders such as early puberty, irregular menstrual cycles, endometriosis, premature ovarian failure, and polycystic ovarian disorder is increasing in parallel with the increasing number of EDCs in the environment.

What this translates to is that endocrine-disrupting environmental toxins such as pesticides and plastic and soy (more on soy and how it negatively impacts your fertility in chapter 5) are disruptive to female hormones and reproduction and are correlated to the increase in reproductive disorders and impaired fertility. Ultimately, this research shows that lifestyle factors are clearly tied to our overall decline in fertility.

Another study, published by the *American Journal of Physiology, Endocrinology, and Metabolism*, states, "Stress-induced reproductive dysfunction is a relatively common cause of infertility in women. In response to everyday life stress, some individuals readily develop reproductive dysfunction (i.e., they are stress sensitive), whereas others are more stress resilient." And what the researchers found was that those who were more stress resilient had an overall "healthier lifestyle"—that is, they were raised lovingly, ate a nutrient-dense diet, got enough sleep, and had a stable social environment.

> Randy Jirtle, an epigenetic researcher from Duke University who studied how certain dietary changes affected the health and longevity of mice (a diet rich in folate, B12, and choline positively influenced health, whereas a diet deficient in those same nutrients caused obesity and disease) said, "My mother told me repeatedly when I was a kid to eat my vegetables and make sure I always ate breakfast. This seems to me to still be sound advice."

An article from the *Proceedings of the National Academy of Sciences of the United States of America* showed that psychological stress causes epigenetic changes that age us faster than is normal. As the authors concluded from their studies, "These findings have implications for understanding how, at the cellular level, stress may promote earlier onset of age-related diseases."

Another paper, published by *Human Genetics* in 2012, discusses how epigenetic changes "are associated with a broad range of disease traits, including cancer, asthma, metabolic disorders, and various reproductive conditions. It seems plausible that changes in epigenetic state may be induced by environmental exposures such as malnutrition, tobacco smoke, air pollutants, metals, organic chemicals, other sources of oxidative stress, and the microbiome, particularly if the exposure occurs during key periods of development. Thus, epigenetic changes could represent an important pathway by which environmental factors influence disease risks, both within individuals and across generations."

What does all of this science actually mean for you and your fertility? That the way you live your life and the environmental toxins and stressors you are exposed to are definitely affecting your health and your fertility (and the health of your future children). Basically, environmental endocrine-disrupting toxins such as pesticides and phytoestrogens (like soy) and stress affect our epigenome, which in turn negatively affects our health and our fertility. Science is telling us that our environment—the pesticide-ridden food we eat, the plastic water bottles we drink out of, the toxic air we breathe, the stress we endure—is decreasing our ability to procreate.

> Environmental toxins (pesticides, plastics, chemicals, stress)→affect our epigeneitcs→cause disease and reproductive disorders.

That's major scientific, Western-based information. It's not likely to be the kind of information any of you are getting from your fertility doctors. You can't really find this information on chat groups, nor is it being discussed by your girlfriends. Nor have I found it in any of the other fertility books on the market. Part of the reason for that is because the epigenetic research is fairly recent (most studies were published in 2010 or later), and another part of the reason is because the Western world puts the biggest credence in our fertility decline as being age-related. However, I think the biggest issue here is that it takes work to make these changes. Our society has gotten dependent on quick fixes. But not you. You are all about rejuvenating your fertility and taking back the power to improve your health.

To reiterate: the way you live your life: the food you eat, the air you breathe, the products you use to clean your house, the makeup and deodorant you use, your stress levels, all have been scientifically shown to affect your fertility.

This may be news to you, but to the world of Traditional Oriental Medicine (TOM) it isn't. According to TOM, "essence" is the crux of our fertility and our health. Essence is the Oriental version of epigenetics. We are each born with a certain amount of essence, which is given to us from our parents (through our genes), and it's meant to last us our whole lives. The amount of essence we are born with determines how long we will live and the health in which we will live. It is also the crux of a woman's ability to sustain life through bearing children, that is, her fertility. Here's the best part: you can build essence. Just like the epigenetics studies showed how negative environmental factors can alter our epigenome and cause genes to turn on or off and adversely impact our health, we can shift our health for the better if we make choices that support our epigenome and our essence. You do this by eating healthfully, living peacefully, sleeping enough, and expressing your emotions.

We can also burn through essence. Too much stress at work, or partying, eating processed and sugar-laden foods, and harboring resentment or anger will use up this essence before it was meant to be used up. Essence declines as we age, just as our bodies age as we grow older. That's just a fact of life. As we age and our essence declines, we get weak and frail, we wrinkle, we become infertile, our hair grays, and we're more susceptible to disease and illness. But what TOM says and Western epigenetic science supports is that the way in which you live your life affects the speed at which you age, that is, the speed at which diseases occur or don't. In TOM we tout: you can use less essence each and every day if you treat your body properly. If you eat well and sleep well and live a balanced and peaceful life, you'll be less toxic and need less of your treasured essence to get through each day. And, you'll be fertile later in life. Our essence and our epigenetics can be affected positively or negatively by how we choose to live our lives. This is great news.

So when you read the statistics that over the age of 35 a woman's fertility significantly declines, you should take into account that there is a BIG difference between your chronological age and your physiological age (and recall from chapter 1 how I showed you science rebutting those statistics). This information doesn't take into account epigenetics or essence. This information doesn't convey to you the power you really have. You have the ability to shift your health and your fertility. Believe in it.

Your Immune System and Your Fertility

Just as Western medical research is discovering that environmental influences are affecting our epigenetics and ultimately hindering our ability to get pregnant, more and more science is also supporting the notion that our immune system also plays an imperative role in our ability to conceive. Most women who come into my practice have what are called "idiopathic" fertility issues, meaning they are having a hard time getting pregnant for "no known reason," according to their doctor's diagnosis. In fact, recent statistics from the Centers For Disease Control state that 30% of all fertility issues are diagnosed as idiopathic. However, what I see in my clinic and what has become a popular topic of discussion among fertility researchers is that a growing portion of these idiopathic cases are actually undiagnosed autoimmune conditions. That's why every element of my fertility rejuvenation program is focused on boosting your immune system and calming any possible autoimmune conditions that could be affecting your ability to get pregnant and carry a pregnancy to term.

Let's break this down: autoimmune disorders result from a problem with your immune system. Normally, your immune system acts as a protector against foreign invaders such as germs, bacteria, and viruses, attacking these foreign invaders to keep us healthy. However, when someone has autoimmunity or an autoimmune disorder, the immune system goes amuck and starts attacking nonforeign body parts, tissues, and organs. Autoimmunity, when activated, for any reason, causes your entire body to be inflamed, stressed, and hostile. Presenting symptoms include: poor digestion, recurring illnesses, skin rashes, blood sugar issues, and difficulty concentrating (see the box "The Most Common Signs of Autoimmunity" on page 50 to see if you have any signs or symptoms of autoimmunity). A body attacking its own tissues is not a hospitable environment for fertility or pregnancy to thrive in. Unfortunately, many women don't receive a diagnosis of their autoimmune disease until they have been trying to conceive without any luck, and some women *never* get a proper diagnosis. (*Note:* It is *really important* if you have an autoimmune disorder to know so *before* you are pregnant, because your autoimmunity can have negative effects on a developing embryo and your pregnancy.)

Autoimmunity has a severely negative impact on fertility. The immune system of women with uncontrolled and undiagnosed autoimmune disorders can attack sperm and embryos, making conception and pregnancy quite difficult. The immune system of a woman with autoimmunity can also attack her ovaries and cause premature ovarian aging (POA) and/or polycystic ovarian syndrome (PCOS); mind you, PCOS is the most common fertility challenge in the United States, affecting approximately 20% to 30% of all women with fertility issues. A 2012 review of current research on this topic was published in the journal *Clinical and Developmental Immunology* and concluded the following, "Autoimmune mechanisms as well as an increased production of multiple autoantibodies are involved in such infertility disorders as premature ovarian failure (POF), endometriosis, polycystic ovary syndrome (PCOS), unexplained infertility, and repeatedly unsuccessful IVF attempts and may be responsible for the pathophysiology of preeclampsia or spontaneous abortions." Said another way: research is showing that autoimmune mechanisms are playing a role in the most common fertility issues woman are facing.

Common Autoimmune Diseases:

Type 1 diabetes
Autoimmune thyroid disease
Celiac disease (CD)
Lupus (SLE)
Rheumatoid arthritis
Scleroderma
Inflammatory bowel disease
Chronic fatigue syndrome
Psoriasis
Multiple sclerosis

If a family member has ever been diagnosed with an autoimmune disease, you too should get screened.

According to the National Institutes of Health (NIH), over the last 10 years the incidence of autoimmune diseases such as type 1 diabetes (which is when your body attacks cells that produce insulin, causing blood sugar issues—it is linked to PCOS) has increased fivefold; celiac disease (CD) (when your body attacks the lining of its own small intestine in response to the ingestion of gluten, a protein that gives bread its airy and fluffy texture and dough its sticky texture—it has been linked to fertility issues) has increased fourfold; and autoimmune thyroid disease (AITD); when your body attacks its own thyroid gland, which in turn throws off all the hormones in your body and nega-tively affects your fertility) has increased to the point where it now affects over 20 million people, 75% of them women. All three of these autoimmune disorders have been scientifically linked to an inability to conceive, which is why the protocol laid out in this book is intentionally geared toward boosting your immune system and calming any autoim-munity that may be going on.

The Most Common Signs of Autoimmunity

Circle the symptoms you experience on a daily basis.)

Extreme fatigue	Low blood sugar	Recurring headaches
Muscle and joint pain	Blood pressure changes	Low-grade fevers
Muscle Weakness	Candida yeast infections	Premenstrual syndrome
Swollen glands		Hair loss
Inflammation	Digestive problems	Recurrent miscarriage
Susceptibility to infections	Anxiety and depression	Thyroid problems
Sleep disturbances	Memory problems	Allergies
Weight loss or gain	Skin rashes	White patches on your skin

Whether you have an autoimmune condition or not, if you are experiencing more than five of these symptoms on a regular basis, there is definitely a good deal of inflammation in your body and it is definitely affecting your ability to conceive. Follow the recommendations in this book and consult with your physician about testing for autoimmune disorders.

Recent research published in the journals *Gynecological Endocrinology* and *Human Reproduction* showed a strong association between endometriosis (the second most common cause of fertil-ity challenges, a condition wherein the tissue that lines the uterus develops outside the uterus, usually on other reproductive organs inside the pelvis or in the abdominal cavity), AITD, and premature ovarian failure, meaning that women typically have all three. Additionally, a study published by *The European Journal of Endocrinology* showed that 27% of women with PCOS (the most common cause of fertility issues) also had AITD. *Polish Endocrinology* published a paper in 2012 concluding that CD, if undiagnosed and untreated, is associated with reproductive disorders, spontaneous abortions, and early menopause. Dr. Sheila Crowe, a professor at the University of Virginia, spoke with *The New York* Times regarding CD and fertility, stating:

> Women with celiac disease are reported to start having periods later and stop menstruating earlier than average. They also suffer more often from secondary amenorrhea, a condition in which menses starts but then stop. Together, these menstrual disorders lead to fewer ovulations, which results in less of a chance to get pregnant. Hormonal factors and poor nutrition are thought to play a role in causing these problems.

The NIH has this statement posted on its website: "In several studies, women with celiac disease who consumed a normal diet (i.e., eating gluten) experienced a shortened reproductive span with delayed onset of menstruation and early menopause, along with more frequent secondary amenorrhea, the temporary or permanent cessation of menstruation in a woman who previously had normal periods. Researchers have found the rate of celiac disease to be 2.5% to 3.5% higher among women with unexplained fertility issues than among women with normal fertility."

To say another way, there is a plethora of current Western medical research that links together the three most common autoimmune diseases—type 1 diabetes, AITD, and CD—and the three top causes of fertility challenges—PCOS, POA, and endometriosis. That's a lot to digest. As one of the reproductive endocrinologists I interviewed for this book, Dr. Hugh Taylor of Yale Reproductive Medicine, said to me, "There is so much more about fertility we don't know than we do know." And Virginia T. Ladd, President and Executive Director of the American Autoimmune Related Diseases Association (AARDA) stated, "With the rapid increase in autoimmune diseases, it clearly suggests that environmental factors (i.e., epigenetics) are at play due to the significant increase in these diseases. Genes do not change in such a short period of time."

Bottom line: environmental factors, such as diet, lifestyle, toxins in our foods and beauty products, and our stress levels are all at play here in the spike of autoimmunity and reproductive issues.

Whether an autoimmune disorder has been diagnosed or not, the diet and lifestyle recommendations I outline in this book will work to quell any autoimmune issue that could be or is currently affecting your fertility. From a Western scientific perspective, the fertility rejuvenation protocol that follows will positively impact your epigenetics and balance your immune system so that pregnancy can occur. From a TOM viewpoint, the plan herein will boost your essence, Qi, and blood, and thereby improve your health and your fertility.

How Long Does It Take for Lifestyle Changes to Have an Impact on Fertility?

One of the most impressive physiological processes the female body is capable of is pregnancy. The process that precedes pregnancy, folliculogenesis, is even more fascinating. Folliculogenesis, which takes place inside your ovaries, is the progression of a number of

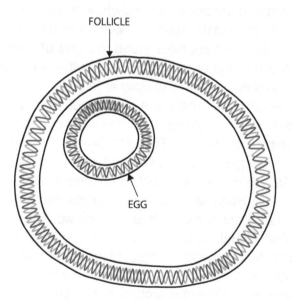

FOLLICLE

EGG

small and immature follicles that grow into large and mature follicles that one day get ovulated. Follicles are defined as a densely packed shell of cells that surrounds an immature egg. When one of these ovulated follicles is fertilized and then is implanted into a lush uterine lining, it becomes an embryo and hopefully a healthy baby. The fascinating part is that these follicles (which surround immature eggs that could one day be your child) have been with us since we were in our own mothers' bellies.

A baby girl growing in her mother's uterus has several million follicles. From the time these follicles are created, at about 20 weeks postconception, they begin degenerating. By the time a girl is born, the number of follicles has dropped from several million to only a few hundred thousand. After birth, the follicles continue to degenerate; this process will continue until there are no follicles (remember, follicles contain our eggs) remaining in the ovary and we are in menopause. From birth to our first menstrual period these follicles just sit there and degenerate. For what purpose, Western science has no known reason. This is one of those "it is what it is" situations.

When a young girl menstruates for the first time, then the process of folliculogenesis begins. Remember, folliculogenesis is the growing and maturing of follicles in your ovary (recall that each follicle contains an egg) and once the process of folliculogenesis is completed, one follicle will ovulate out an egg that can potentially become your baby.

The entire process of folliculogenesis takes about 365 days, and it's continuous, meaning that at any time the ovary contains follicles in all stages of development. Keep in mind, folliculogenesis is about the growth and maturation of follicles (that contain one egg each) from the pool of follicles you were born with, from the pool of follicles that is continuously degenerating. Each month your ovary recruits several follicles from this pool to grow and mature, but only *one* of those several follicles will actually be the chosen one that will ovulate out its egg. All the other ones that were maturing will die off, further depleting your pool of follicles. With each ovulatory cycle, one follicle (called the dominant follicle) releases an egg that can be fertilized, and the other follicles that were maturing start to wither away.

Folliculogenesis takes 365 days, but for the purpose of discussing fertility rejuvenation all we really care about are the last 100 or so days of the process. This is called the preantral phase of folliculogenesis. But for simplicity, let's just call this phase the "affected by your lifestyle" phase. The "affected by your life-style" phase contains growing and maturing follicles that are about 100 days away from being ovulated. Why do we care about this "affected by your lifestyle" phase so much? Because it is at this point that the follicles in your ovaries are responsive to the hormones in your body and are affected by your lifestyle.

You see, up until this stage, the follicles in your body were not responsive to your hormones. They just did their thing independent of what hormones were slushing around in your body. But, now these follicles are maturing and developing at a fast rate and they need nutrients from your body to do so. This dependence on nutrients from your body means the follicles are more affected by what's going on inside that body of yours. Say you are managing your stress well, sleeping enough, eating loads of organic nutrient-dense foods, then your follicles are developing in a hormonally and emotionally balanced environment and will likely create a better-quality egg that can one day become your baby. However, for example, if you're eating too much estrogen-producing soy, or conventionally raised animals that are pumped with hormones, or testosterone-stimulating sugar and white flour, or you're in a flight-or-fight constantly stressed-out mode, these follicles are affected and will likely produce a poorer-quality egg that may not be ideal for sustaining pregnancy.

Follicles that are about 100 or so days away from being ovulated can be affected by the way you live your life, that is, the food you eat, how much you sleep, the stress you endure, the chemicals you are (or are not) exposed to.

What this means for you: *we need to start rejuvenating our fertility for at least three months before we can affect the quality of our eggs.* That means you need to follow the fertility rejuvenation protocol outlined in this book for at least three months before you can effectively rejuvenate your fertility.

What is vital to understand to help improve your fertility is that from about 100 days prior to ovulation your developing follicles (and the eggs they contain) are affected by not just the hormones your body is releasing, but also the internal environment in which they are growing. This is when the positive or negative epigenetic changes or the abundance or lack of essence can make its mark. So to be redundant, if that internal environment is happy and balanced and full of healthy nutrients you're making a good-quality egg. Alternatively, if that internal environment is Qi-less and loaded with toxic chemicals, stress, anxiety, anger, preservatives, and additives, you're not making a great-quality egg.

In 2009, the journal *Seminars in Reproductive Medicine* published an article stating: "Because epigenetic reprogramming occurs during folliculogenesis and embryogenesis (the development of an embryo), any disturbance of the normal natural environment during these critical phases could cause epigenetic alterations."

Another research article published in a 2013 issue of *Cell Metabolism* states: "Follicle loss can be dramatically accelerated by external insults, including chemotherapy, radiation, and environmental toxins, leading to the premature onset of many health problems associated with natural menopause."

What this research indicates is that environmental influences such as the food you eat, the emotional state you exist in, and the environmental toxins you have been exposed to for the last 100 or so days, can impact directly your epigenetics and the development and growth of the follicle that contains the egg that you hope to become your baby.

This is why I am here to educate you on how to rejuvenate your fertility, not just for the three months before you ovulate but for your life. The approach I have outlined in this book will not only improve your fertility, it will improve your overall health.

Over the next several chapters, I'll cover the four main areas of the fertility rejuvenation plan:

1. Becoming one with nature and regaining your body's balance
2. Eating for optimal nutrition and egg quality
3. Steering clear of environmental toxins
4. Preparing yourself mentally and emotionally

I will go over this plan in step-by-step detail, making it easy for you to live the fertility rejuvenation way. Your new lifestyle will positively influence your epigenetics, immune system, and your three vital treasures: essence, Qi, and blood, and will improve your health and your fertility.

In the next chapter, we will explore what it means to become one with nature and why it is fundamental to fertility rejuvenation. Before you turn the page, take a moment to repeat your mantra:

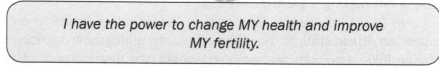

I have the power to change MY health and improve MY fertility.

Yes, you do!

Part II
The Fertility Rejuvenation Plan

4
Becoming One with Nature: Regaining Your Body's Balance

One major guiding principle of Traditional Oriental Medicine (TOM) philosophy is that a body that is one with nature smoothly transitions through life's stages with balance, health, and peace. When I say, *a body that is one with nature*, I don't mean that you have to pack up and move to the woods somewhere, although having interaction with nature is part of this notion. The concept of becoming one with nature is more of a spiritual one, implying that a body that is in touch with nature is a body that is in touch with its own physical and emotional states, is aware of its own natural rhythms and how the surrounding environment affects it, and has a sense of peace in knowing it is part of a larger universe. It's a body that is present in its daily life and aware of how it is adversely affected by too little sleep, overindulging in junk food, or stressful situations.

If that doesn't sound like you at the present moment, no worries. That's what I am here for, and this chapter will guide you in simple ways to become more in touch with the nature of your body.

For my fertility clients (and for you after you apply the information in this chapter and the rest of the book), a body that is one with nature is brimming with fertility. When your health and your reproductive system and all its parts are working in accordance with the natural rhythms of your body, it should be menstruating monthly, ovulating in a timely manner, and maintaining a pristine hormonal balance, all with ease and efficiency. When your reproductive system is going with the flow of nature, there are very few issues or concerns. When your body and its reproductive system aren't one with your environment, you know it: you have an irregular period, either coming too early, too late, or not at all; you are a bag of emotions premenstrually; you get hormonal acne; you have no desire for sex; your body swells two pant sizes the week before your period is due; you're having trouble getting pregnant and you don't see healthy, fertile cervical mucus during ovulation. Additionally, your health is out of balance in other ways: your sleep is not restful, your digestion is off, your energy is low, your skin is dry, and your immune system is weak. Basically, a body that is not one with nature is a body that is not as healthy as it should be.

In order for you to get a more solid understanding of the TOM tenet that a body that is one with nature smoothly transitions through life's stages with balance, health, and peace, I want to take you on a journey back about 2,000 years to China. We are going to eavesdrop on a conversation between a Chinese emperor known as the Yellow Emperor and his physician named Qi Bo. This conversation comes from the oldest extant text in TOM, *The Yellow Emperor's Classic of Internal Medicine*. This book is considered one of the most important texts on Taoism and TOM, discussing health and disease prevention and the importance of living life in accordance with nature.

The Yellow Emperor clears his throat and asks Qi Bo, "I've heard that in the days of old everyone lived 100 years without showing the usual signs of aging. In our time, however, people age prematurely, living only 50 years. Is this due to a change in the environment, or is it because people have lost the correct way of life?"

Qi Bo takes a deep breath, sips his tea, and begins speaking, "In the past, people practiced the Tao, the Way of Life. They understood the principle of balance as represented by the transformations of the energies of the universe. They formulated exercises to promote energy flow to harmonize themselves with the universe.

They ate a balanced diet at regular times, arose and retired at regular hours, avoided overstressing their bodies and minds, and refrained from overindulgence of all kinds. They maintained well-being of body and mind; thus, it is not surprising that they lived over 100 years."

Qi Bo runs his fingers through his long beard and continues, "These days, people have changed their way of life. They drink wine as though it were water, indulge excessively in destructive activities, drain their kidney essence and deplete their Qi. They do not know the secret of conserving their energy and vitality. Seeking emotional excitement and momentary pleasures, people disregard the natural rhythm of the universe. They fail to regulate their lifestyle and diet and sleep improperly. So, it is not surprising that they look old at 50 and die soon after."

Coming back to the present day, let's break down this conversation: if you nourish your body with healthy and nutrient-dense foods, get enough sleep, avoid overindulgence as much as possible, live with the seasons, and keep your emotional life peaceful and happy, you can preserve your essence and remain healthy, vital, and fertile until much later in life. In fact, this same book states that a woman will remain fertile until the age of 49 so long as she secures her essence and lives her life in harmony with nature. For you, living in the 21st century, remaining fertile way into your 40s has everything to do with living in balance with nature and preserving your essence.

Ask yourself these questions:

- Do you have a stress-free life?
- Do you sleep enough?
- Do you regularly eat nutrient-dense foods such as farm fresh eggs (with the yolk) and grass-fed animal liver?
- Do you let your body rest on the first day of your period?
- Do you seek joy in your life on a daily basis?
- Do you avoid eating frozen, cold, and/or raw foods in the middle of winter?
- Do you get outside and take in nature daily?

Answering no to any one of these questions tells me that you are not living in balance and are unnecessarily burning up your essence and negatively impacting your epigenetics and immune system. The rest of this chapter, and much of this book, will walk you through some basics on forming a kinship with nature so that you can have an abundant essence and get your health and your fertility in tune with nature.

Your Long Lost Friend: Nature

Most of us don't take time each day to tune into our bodies, to see how we feel, to see if we are tired or rested or tense or over-caffeinated. We have not only lost touch with nature, as in grass and trees and sunshine and moonlight, but we have also lost touch with the nature of ourselves. A huge part of rejuvenating your fertility is about getting in touch with the rhythm of your body and how it interacts with its natural environment. It is imperative to take time and tune into your body.

For instance: How do you feel when you wake up in the morning? Do you feel rested? Are you hungry? Do you have a bowel movement first thing upon waking?

Or how do you feel as you're heading to work? Are you anxious, tense, excited? Are you present in your daily life or do you just move from one task to the next until your day is over and then do it all over again the next day?

As an individual functioning in our modern society, there is so much we do without thinking, without being conscious or present. We just wake up, hop out of bed, rush to the shower, turn on the computer, and check our e-mail. We go to bed watching TV (according to Neilsen numbers, the average American watches 34 hours of TV per week) with our phones next to us, and we look at our messages just before retiring to sleep and immediately after we awake. Do you ever wonder how this constant interaction with electronics is having an effect on our health?

For almost all of human history, until very recently, we were outdoors, in nature, taking in vitamin D–loaded natural sunlight (vitamin D, a fat-soluble vitamin, is imperative for healthy fertility; more on that in chapter 5) and hunting and gathering our food. Over the last 100 years, as we have become more urbanized, we have lost touch with this interaction with nature. At present, most all of our environments are artificial; some days we don't even see the outdoors. Granted, over the last 100 years, some major strides in hygiene and survival have been made, and as a population we are living longer than ever before (think vaccines, clean running water, and antibiotics). However, we are also dealing with more disease than ever before, and science has shown that our lack of interaction with the outdoors and our increasingly chronic exposure to electronics and artificial environments that are devoid of nature is having detrimental effects on our health.

In 2013, the *International Journal of Environmental Research and Public Health* compiled nearly a century of research surrounding the positive effects of human interaction with nature and concluded:

> Interacting with nature may therefore be important not only for survival, but also for human quality of life. Indeed, there is mounting empirical evidence that interacting with nature delivers a range of measurable human benefits, including positive effects on physical health, psychological well-being, cognitive ability and social cohesion.

Research published in Oxford's *Health Promotion International* journal in 2006 discussed whether too much "artificial stimulation and an existence spent in purely human environments may cause exhaustion or produce a loss of vitality and health."

Another publication, *The Experience of Nature: A Psychological Perspective* from Cambridge University Press, states, "People with access to nearby natural settings have been found to be healthier overall than other individuals. The longer-term, indirect impacts (of 'nearby nature') also include increased levels of satisfaction with one's home, one's job, and with life in general."

Seems like Qi Bo was onto something when he commented on how those who disregard nature look old at 50 and die soon after. Just as the Western science of epigenetics has caught up with the TOM theory of postnatal essence (meaning our genetics are not set in stone and the way we live our life determines our health and vitality) it also now supports Qi Bo's 2, 000-year-old notion that humans need to be in touch with the natural rhythm of their environment for their health to not only prevail but to flourish.

When it comes to fertility rejuvenation, our goal is to get your health in optimal condition so that your fertility will be primed and ready to go when you are. A big piece to that is getting you back in touch with your body, its natural rhythms, and nature. A cornerstone to rejuvenating your fertility is living in the flow of nature.

Living in the Flow of Nature

Admittedly, my life is just as modernized as yours. I am on my laptop and my smartphone a big chunk of the day in between seeing and caring for patients. However, I make sure to find ways to stay in touch with my body, its natural rhythm, and nature during the day. I am going to share these easy strategies with you. It's not that hard to live in the flow of nature. We talked in chapter 2 about how your fertile body works from a Western and an Eastern perspective. Now you need to know what to do on a daily basis in order to keep it working optimally, to keep your HPO axis pumping out the right amount of hormones *at the right time*, and to keep your three vital substances (essence, Qi, and blood) abundant so that you can get pregnant and stay pregnant.

First, here are the top 10 signs that your health is out of the flow with nature and what it should feel like when it is in touch with that flow:

1. You wake up tired or groggy and all you want to do is sleep more. *What to strive for:* You should wake feeling rested and energetic.
2. You get headaches on a regular basis, from tension or fatigue or perhaps you don't know the reason why. *What to strive for:* No pain. Anywhere.
3. You have bad PMS cramps, bloating, acne, and mood swings. *What to strive for:* Minor cramping with slight breast tenderness and little to no moodiness.
4. You are having difficulty conceiving. *What to strive for:* Pregnancy within the first 6 to 12 months of attempting to conceive.
5. You have digestive complaints such as gas, bloating, reflux, constipation, and/or diarrhea. *What to strive for:* No bloat, no reflux, very infrequent gas, and an easy-to-pass, formed bowel movement one to two times daily.
6. You experience anxiety or depression regularly. *What to strive for:* Happiness, gratitude, and optimism, with the occasional situational "upset" that you can bounce right back from.

7. You are easily frustrated and irritated. *What to strive for:* A chilled-out, go-with-the-flow attitude.
8. You have a poor sex drive. *What to strive for:* A regular desire for sex with a noticeable increase in sex drive during ovulation.
9. You have weak or brittle nails, thinning hair, or dry skin. *What to strive for:* Healthy, strong, and hydrated hair, nails, and skin.
10. You get colds easily or with every change of the season. *What to strive for:* A strong immune system that can fight off colds. A cold once or twice per year is acceptable.

Even if you only experience a few of these out-of-the-flow-with-nature symptoms, you will benefit from the following advice to help your body become one with nature, your health, and your fertility, so you can thrive.

> "There is some evidence that before the age of artificial lighting, birth control pills, and working indoors, women all ovulated in sync with the phases of the moon," says Joyce Stahmann, MPH, a fertility educator and professional herbalist in Portland, Oregon, who teaches the Natural Fertility Management Program.

Here are the 10 things you need to start doing *now* to become one with nature and optimize your fertility:

1. Sleep seven to eight hours each night. Science shows that sleep affects your fertility hormones such as FSH, LH, estrogen, and progesterone. If you are lacking the proper amount of sleep for optimal functioning hormones, menstrual cycles and fertility will suffer.
2. Eat protein regularly (every two to three hours) and eat foods as close to their natural state as possible (I will get into this in great detail in the next chapter).
3. Achieve a fertile weight. Your weight can be a big culprit when it comes to a dysfunctional female reproductive system as fat cells store estrogen and estrogen is a majorly important hormone in an efficient female reproductive system. So if you have too little *or* too much fat, it will completely disrupt your estrogen levels and affect your ability to get pregnant. If a woman is underweight she typically has a low percentage of body fat and

doesn't have enough estrogen to generate a regular menstrual cycle, let alone get pregnant. Alternatively, when a woman is overweight, she has excess estrogen (as estrogen is stored in fat cells), which completely disrupts the body's ability to carry out a normal menstruation and ovulation. Excess estrogen also predisposes women to illnesses such as endometriosis, polycystic ovarian syndrome, breast cancer, and uterine fibroids— all of which will significantly hinder one's chances of becoming pregnant. That is why I recommend you maintain a healthy body mass index (BMI) that is between 18.5 and 24.9 (see the box on how to figure out your BMI).

Determining Your BMI

Plug your weight and height into this formula: weight (lb) / [height (in)]^2 × 703

---

4. Exercise four to five days each week. Too much or too little exercise can really affect your fertility. However, exercise, like weight, is a hard issue to make definitive recommendations about, as everyone's body is so entirely different. My general rule of thumb is four to five days per week of at least 30 minutes of exercise. The level of intensity depends upon your comfort level and your goals. If you have a high BMI and are looking to lose weight to optimize your fertility quotient, then some heart-pounding, sweat-soaking workouts may be what you need. On the other hand, if you are a long distance runner and need to put on some weight, then I recommend you adopt some less intense means of exercise such as restorative yoga or walking.

   Bottom line: exercise is imperative to optimal health, but like everything else you must find a natural balance with it.

5. Get outside every single day for sunlight and fresh air. For optimal hormonal balance and HPO axis function, get two 10-minute doses of unprotected sunlight each day. If you have a beach or a park nearby, make it a plan to get there (and bring your partner) often. If you have a backyard filled with trees, drink your morning tea (or organic coffee) out there. If you live near a forest, take a walk and soak up the scenery.

> Here's a challenge for you: spend more time outside in one week than you do watching television (even if it's cold out).

6. Grow a garden and fill your house with plants. It is understandable that sometimes getting outside every day can be a challenge, so bring nature inside. Science shows that indoor plants boost moods, reduce anxiety and depression, and improve air quality.

7. Turn off your electronics one hour before bed. This is a big one. My general recommendation is that an hour before bedtime the TV is off, the smartphone is off (and being charged outside of your bedroom), your laptop is off, and your tablet or iPad is off. If there is a TV in your bedroom, remove it (I'm dead serious). Your bedroom is for sleep and sex. When you get into bed, read a real book, journal about your thoughts or your day, talk with your partner, have sex, meditate, or all of the above. Turn electronics off. If your phone is your alarm clock then go out and buy a battery-operated alarm and keep it in your bedroom (it will come in handy if there is a power outage).

8. Meditate. I often refer to meditation as chill-out time, as that's really what it is—a time to sit, breathe, and chill out. To get back in touch with nature, I want you to do the following: take

> Meditation, or chilling-out, or sitting and breathing, or whatever you want to call It, Is imperative to becoming one with the nature of your body. Here's a brief how-to:
>
> - Sit comfortably, relax your shoulders, rest your hands on your lap, palms up toward the sky.
> - Close your eyes and take deep, belly-rising breaths. The breathing cycle should be: deep breath in (3–4 seconds), belly rise, hold for a count of 2 seconds, then a long slow exhale (again, 3–4 seconds).
>
> For more meditation assistance, check out my "How to Meditate" video on YesICanGetPregnant.com.

five minutes each day to meditate, chill out, sit, breathe, and check in with your body's natural rhythm. You can do this while you are sitting outside soaking up some sunshine or at your desk. And don't forget to practice your child's palace mantra from chapter 1 every single morning, right after you wake up and before you get out of bed: *Dear Uterus, you are the palace of my child and I believe in you. I send you love and joy. You are a beautiful palace, brimming with fertility, and I fully believe in your ability to get pregnant.*

9. Have HOT Sex! Did you forget that sex is fun and should be enjoyed? Losing touch with the nature of lust that was once a part of your relationship is not an uncommon predicament to be in when your primary focus is baby-making. However, keeping sex sexy is not just important for your relationship or your baby-making, it is also fun and feels so good. You and your partner both deserve to have fun, feel good, and enjoy hot sex with each other. Try your best to get back to the nature of spontaneous and hot sex by tuning into your desire to be with your partner. Every day, take a moment and recall a time when you couldn't keep your hands off your partner and remind yourself of the reasons you find him sexy. And don't forget to find ways to make yourself feel sexy and irresistible. When you feel irresistible, you are, and your partner won't be able to keep his hands off you!

10. Keep Your Child's Palace Warm. A warm uterus is a fertile uterus. In TOM we often diagnose fertility patients with something called a "cold uterus," which literally means the uterus it out of touch with its natural state and is too cold to foster a life. Often, this means there is not enough healthy blood flow to your child's palace or there is stagnant blood in your child's palace—sometimes both. Here are some tips that I want to remind you to do *all the time* to maintain the natural rhythm of your child's palace:

- Do not sit too much or too often on cold and wet floors or chairs.
- Keep warm in the feet, stomach, and back areas. Wear clothes that cover the navel and back. Wear socks or stockings and shoes in cold weather.

- Do not swim during the menstrual period.
- Dry your hair after showering before going out.
- Try not to drink cold drinks, including water, or eat frozen food, especially during your menstrual period. (Do not drink cold drinks on an empty stomach.)

There you have it, 10 tips on getting your body back in touch with its own natural rhythms. Follow these tips *daily* and know that a body that is in touch with nature is healthy and fertile.

Getting in Touch with the Seasons

In order to understand the importance of our ever-changing seasons here on earth, and regardless of where you live, even if the weather is always balmy, you still experience seasonal changes. Let's see what our wise friend Qi Bo has to say: "The changes of the four seasons is the root of life, growth, reproduction, aging, and destruction. By respecting this natural law it is possible to live free from illness. The sages have followed this, and the foolish people have not." So how does one go about "respecting" this natural law of the seasons? The changes of the four seasons are not only present in the obvious way, they are also present in our monthly menstrual cycle. You see, there are also four phases to your menstrual cycle. I know we talked a little bit about these phases in chapter 2, but let's discuss them again:

- **Menstruation:** when you are actually bleeding
- **Follicular phase:** when the follicles in your ovaries gradually grow
- **Ovulation:** when a mature follicle ruptures and can potentially become fertilized by sperm
- **Luteal phase:** the time when the uterine lining continues to build up and either becomes home to a little embryo or prepares to shed itself to begin the cycle again

Each phase of your menstrual cycle corresponds to the four seasons of the year: winter, spring, summer, and fall. Okay, let's break this down further and give you some tips on respecting the seasonal laws of your body's monthly cycle.

Menstruation Phase

In TOM we see the menstruation phase correlating with the season of winter. The reason why is that winter is the most inactive time of year. It is when things contract and become dormant. In the same way, during the menstruation phase of our cycles, our hormones are the most inactive they are all month, and the uterus is shedding its lining much like trees shed their leaves in winter. During this phase of your cycle (and in the wintertime as well) it is best to:

- **Reflect.** Be introspective and journal about the past month. Cleanse out any emotions you are holding on to that don't serve you, like the sadness or anger you felt when you got your period *again* this month.
- **Rest.** Often, during our menstrual cycle we tend to be tired as our body is giving up blood. So listen to your body and rest. Instead of intense exercise, practice yoga or tai chi. Qi Bo says during the winter phase we should go to bed early and rise late. Listen to him. Rest is really important during this time.
- **Nourish.** As discussed earlier, the kidneys house our precious essence. In TOM the kidneys are also the organ that corresponds to winter. During this time when you are menstruating it's important to eat warming foods such as hearty soups and red meat and sip on ginger tea. (In the next chapter, I will go into greater detail on nutrition and what to eat for optimum fertility.) It's important to nourish yourself from an emotional perspective, too. Take some more time than usual to meditate, and be sure to find time each day to look in the mirror and find something beautiful about yourself.

In the season of winter, it is best to:

- Get to bed early (10:00 p.m.) and wake up late (7:00 a.m.) in the morning when the sun is shining.
- Mentally, be quiet and reflective. Meditation is important this time of year.
- Practice light physical exercise.

(continued)

(*continued*)

> • Protect your body against the cold by keeping warm,
> but not too hot; it is important to avoid overheating and
> sweating during this time of year.
> • Eat cooked foods such as beef stew and chicken soup
> with spices such as ginger and cinnamon.

Follicular Phase

The follicular phase, which starts as your menstrual flow is slowing down (around cycle day 3 or 4 where day 1 is the first day of bleeding), is associated with the season of spring. Spring is the time of revitalization and birth. Flowers bloom, grass grows, and there is hope in the air. This is the start of a new menstrual cycle. Follicles begin to grow and the potential of a baby in nine or so months is looming. During this phase of your menstrual cycle, it is best to:

- **Aspire.** Be ambitious. Make a list of five things you hope will happen in the coming month. Make another list of five things that you are most grateful for at this moment in time.
- **Move.** Get out and take a walk or go for a run. This is a great time for cardio, so move your body. Don't forget to stretch. For you liver and heart blood-deficient ladies, no running for you; rather do some Vinyasa yoga or go for a brisk walk.
- **Breathe.** Take in deep breaths and let out long exhales. In TOM the liver is the organ associated with the season of spring and deep breaths with long exhales. Make a sighing noise while you exhale; it really frees up the liver energy. Be sure not to suppress any emotions in this phase as that will delay ovulation.

> In the season of spring, it is important to:
>
> • Get to bed late (11:00 p.m.) and awaken early (6:00 a.m.).
> • Exercise briskly in the morning.
> • Enliven the mind and give birth to new desires.
> • Maintain an even, calm state of mind and express your emotions.
> • Eat fresh green foods such as sprouts, kale, spinach, and dandelion.

Ovulation Phase

Ovulation matches the energy of the summer. This is when things get hot and heavy, and that's exactly what you and your partner should be doing if you want a baby. This is when things are in full bloom, both in nature and in your ovaries. Your body is about to release a mature egg that can hopefully be fertilized and become your baby. If you are currently charting your basal body temperatures, this is the time when your internal temperature spikes, just like the outside temperature spikes in the summer. During this phase it is best to:

- **Create.** Make things happen, in the bedroom and out of the bedroom. Get your creative juices flowing: draw or sing or dance, or do them all.
- **Laugh.** Find joy wherever you can. Be playful. This is a time for living to the fullest. The summer season is related to the heart, and, as you know from chapter 1, the heart loves joy. Make yourself and your heart happy and get out to do something you love. Avoid anger at all costs.
- **Receive.** Be open and receptive, not just emotionally, but physically. Be open to the idea of receiving new life in your womb. This is a good time to do some fertility-enhancing yoga poses and Qi Gong exercises (which we will discuss in chapter 9)

In the season of summer, it is important to:

- Get to bed late (11:00 p.m.) and wake up early (6:00 a.m.)
- Realize our life's greatest potential and go after your dreams.
- Keep a cheerful state of mind and avoid anxiety and anger.
- Get outside and exercise in the morning and take a rest mid-day.
- Stay hydrated and eat foods such as cucumber, watermelon, bok choy, and asparagus. Avoid heavy, greasy, fried foods.

Luteal Phase

The luteal phase is likened to the season of autumn or fall. This is the time of harvest when we gather to prepare for winter. As your uterine lining thickens and you are either pregnant or not, your body in this phase is holding and preparing for what is next. It is best to do the following during this phase:

- **Chill.** Stay calm and tranquil. Meditate and let go of any negative emotions. Visualize an embryo nestling up inside your thickened uterine lining, or even better, visualize yourself pregnant.

A Luteal Phase Visualization

Lie flat on your back, place your hands over your lower abdomen, and while breathing in and out nice and slowly visualize a baby cozily nestling up in the warmth and radiance of your child's palace. Try to spend three to five minutes lying still, breathing, and visualizing your child's palace with a growing baby inside of it. Imagine how that would feel. Think about how excited you would be, how much love you would feel, how truly blessed you would feel to be housing a precious life.

Visualization is a powerful tool that I encourage you to use, especially during your luteal phase. More on this in chapter 7.

- **Prepare.** Organize your thoughts, your home, your plans. This is a good time to ready yourself for what is next. Take that list you created during your follicular phase and start making plans on how to achieve those desires.
- **Nibble.** Eat foods that are orange or red, such as yams and beets. They will help balance your body and your hormones (e.g., progesterone) during the luteal phase as these foods are very nourishing to the spleen energy. In TOM, it is the spleen's energy that is responsible for holding a pregnancy once conception has occurred.

In the season of autumn, or fall, it is important to:

- Get to bed early (10:00 p.m.) and awaken early (6:00 a.m.).
- Get organized, finish projects, and become more introspective.
- Keep your mind in a peaceful, chill state and let go of any negative emotions.

(*continued*)

- Exercise moderately and practice deep breathing.
- Eat fewer uncooked foods and more cooked foods such as steamed broccoli, Brussels sprouts, and yams.

Now that you have the know-how to abide with the natural laws of the seasons during each phase of your cycle, you can work with nature to regulate your cycle, be more fertile, and get in touch with the natural rhythms of your body and your environment. Living in accordance with nature and detaching from the modern, electronically inclined world will benefit both your health and your fertility. Apply all of the recommendations in this chapter and get your body in the flow of nature—your fertility will thrive. Now turn the page and let's get into the best dietary advice for rejuvenating your fertility.

5
Eating for Optimal Nutrition and Egg Quality: The *Yes, You Can Get Pregnant* Diet

Jan, a 33-year-old corporate lawyer, came to me a week after her second unsuccessful intrauterine insemination (IUI). She was very upset and unsettled. A year prior she had gotten pregnant the second month she and her husband tried, but she miscarried after six weeks. Since that miscarriage Jan has been completely focused on getting pregnant. As she sipped on her bottle of diet iced tea, she told me her story. From my intake I gathered that she had a history of fertility-reducing eating habits. Her diet consisted of processed, low-fat, sugar-free, artificially sweetened, pesticide-ridden food *stuff*. There wasn't a single nutrient-dense food in her diet.

When we started talking about the imperative role her diet plays in her fertility she looked at me as if I had two heads. Unfortunately, I see this type of reaction all too much. The food we eat directly affects everything concerning fertility in our bodies, from the eggs we ovulate to the thickness of our child's palace uterine lining, the abundance of essence-rich blood flow to our reproductive organs, the amount of PMS we experience each month, and the regularity of our periods.

To effectively rejuvenate your fertility, know this: *The food you eat affects your fertility.*

Recent scientific research, presented at the Annual Clinical Meeting of The American College of Obstetricians and Gynecologists by Dr. Jeffrey Russel, showed that a protein-rich diet is essential for good-quality embryos and better egg quality. As well, research out of Harvard University has shown that full-fat dairy products are better for fertility than low-fat ones, that a high-protein and low-carb diet improved fertility, and that women who avoid trans fats and simple sugars are more fertile than those who do not. Several scientific articles have shown that antioxidants such as vitamins A, C, and E ward off oxidative stress (another term for premature aging) and improve both male and female fertility, thus influenceing viable pregnancy rates. In addition, other research has directly linked pesticides in non-organic foods to reproductive disorders, and in animal studies, the dietary intake of genetically modified (GM) foods not only caused fertility issues but sterility, autoimmune diseases, certain cancers, and accelerated aging.

Now, let's talk about the Traditional Oriental Medicine (TOM) point of view on food. In TOM, when it comes to health and fertility, Qi is a very important substance (along with blood and essence). We talked about Qi a few times already, but let me recap: Qi is the building block of life, the core of health and vitality. Qi is life force. The number one place we get our Qi from is the foods we eat.

Think of an organic, shiny red apple growing in a beautiful apple orchard: that's a food filled with Qi. Now imagine a plastic, pasteurized, packaged applesauce foodstuff with added synthetic vitamins, food coloring, and high fructose corn syrup purchased in a fluorescent lit store: that's a dead foodstuff that has no Qi.

For 5000 years, TOM has preached the necessity of eating a diet full of life-giving, nutrient-dense, and Qi-rich foods which maximizes overall health, including fertility, by improving the quality of your entire reproductive system: your uterus, ovaries, fallopian tubes, menstrual cycle, and, most importantly, the eggs that you ovulate each month.

Eating Qi-rich foods fills you with an abundance of Qi that leads to vibrant health and optimal fertility; alternatively, a shortage of Qi leaves you ill and fragile, and greatly reduces your chances of getting pregnant or even ovulating healthy fertile eggs

> *Repeat after me:*
> I have the power to change MY health and improve
> MY fertility.

each month. *Translation:* without ample and healthy Qi there can be no pregnancy.

You see, foods filled with Qi give you fresh and fertility-enhancing nutrients, essential vitamins and minerals, and healthy fats that bring your hormones into balance, improves the quality of the eggs in your ovaries, and makes it optimal for you to get pregnant.

The quality of the egg your body ovulates each month is a direct function of the internal environment in your body and the amount of healthy Qi you have. If you are not eating nutrient-dense, wholesome, clean, and organic foods, the chances of your eggs being superb quality are slim. If you recall our discussion about the process of folliculogenesis from chapter 2, the quality of the egg you are about to ovulate this month has been directly influenced by the nutrients (or lack of) you have put in your body over the last 100 or so days.

So how do you get superb-quality eggs?

Follow the *Yes, You Can Get Pregnant* diet for at least three months, but preferably forever. The *Yes, You Can Get Pregnant* diet will radically shift how you think about food, your health, your body, your fertility, and the relationship between them all. It is intended as a lifestyle change, *not* as a diet fad that you follow for a few weeks.

The *Yes, You Can Get Pregnant* Diet

Just as becoming one with nature will help rejuvenate your fertility, so will the *Yes, You Can Get Pregnant* diet. The diet may require you to do some things you might not normally do such as read labels, buy organic for the important items, and cook and eat lots of saturated fat (yes, fat!), but by doing all of this you will be eating delicious food and cultivating healthy Qi and abundant energy so that your body will be in the best shape possible to nurture life. This fertility-rejuvenating lifestyle has the added bonuses of radiant skin, deeper sleep, emotional stability, a rockin' sex drive, and a leaner body.

General Guidelines

- Eat more cooked food than raw food. By raw I mean foods that are cold and/or not cooked. There is a reason for this: in TOM cold or raw foods are hard to digest and therefore hard to get healthy, abundant, and fertile Qi from. We say in TOM that cold and raw foods make for a cold uterus, and a cold uterus is not a fertile one. So, when following this plan, be sure that you are eating most of your foods cooked. That doesn't mean you can't have a vegetable juice now and again, just have it in moderation.
- Vegetables should be fresh, organic (when necessary, see list on page 83), and lightly steamed or sautéed in a healthy fat (as mentioned on page 85).
- Animal products should be certified organic and pasture-raised or grass-fed.

For resources on where to buy certified organic, pasture-raised or grass-fed animal products, visit www.YesICanGetPregnant.com.

The Six Big No's

There are six big no's that you will need to follow without exceptions. No cheating or believing that "just a little won't hurt" (because it will!).

No Gluten

Several research articles published in prestigious journals such as *The Journal of Reproductive Medicine* and *Fertility and Sterility* have reported an association between celiac disease (CD) or gluten intolerance and fertility issues with an increased risk of miscarriage. It is speculated that this occurs because gluten aggravates your immune system, which results in those with either CD or gluten intolerance having malabsorption issues so that they are in turn deficient in several vitamins and minerals, namely iron, folic acid, and vitamins D and K, all of which are essential for pregnancy.

Said another way: gluten not only is inflammatory and activates autoimmunity in your body, but it also is extremely difficult to digest—eating it will compromise your ability to digest and absorb nutrients from *any* other foods you eat. Therefore, based on the current research, I strongly encourage all of my fertility patients to avoid gluten. *By avoid, I mean you cannot eat gluten.* Even a small amount of gluten here and there will aggravate and inflame your body and your immune system will attack your precious tissues and organs (including your reproductive organs).

Gluten, the protein typically found in wheat, barley, and rye grains, also hides out in the following foods:

Spelt	Kamut	Durum	Beauty products (e.g., shampoo, lipstick, face creams)
Einkorn	Semolina	Couscous	
Seitan	Bulgur	Farina	
Emmer	Matzo	Graham	Triticale
Soy sauce	Communion wafers	vegetarian mock meats	Wheat germ
MSG (monosodium glutamate)	Processed meats		Faro
Textured vegetable protein (TVP)	Some store-bought broths (read labels!)	Marinades/ sauces	bouillon cubes

When you avoid gluten, you need to avoid all of the above foodstuffs as well.

No Genetically Modified (GM) Foods

In addition to gluten-containing grains being linked to autoimmune diseases and fertility issues, there is growing evidence that all the GM food in our diet is also negatively affecting our fertility and our autoimmunity. To be clear, gluten-containing grains such as wheat, barley, and rye have been chemically altered, which is different (and some argue, worse) than the genetic modification of foods such as corn and soy. GM foods contain organisms or species that have been altered, manipulated, and designed in a laboratory, and foreign genes, such as viruses or bacteria, have been inserted into them so that they can grow in spite of bugs and inclement weather. Approximately 80% of foods sold in supermarkets are genetically modified, and nearly all of the corn, soy, and canola in this country is genetically modified. GM foods have been linked to hormonal and reproductive issues in many scientific studies. According to the American Academy of Environmental Medicine, "There is more than a casual association between GM foods and adverse health effects. The strength of association and consistency between GM foods and disease is confirmed in several animal studies. Multiple animal studies show significant immune dysregulation associated with asthma, allergy, and inflammation. Animal studies also show altered structure and function of the liver as well as cellular changes that could lead to accelerated aging. A recent 2008 study links GM corn with infertility, showing a significant decrease in offspring over time and significantly lower litter weight in mice fed GM corn. This study also found that over 400 genes were found to be expressed differently in the mice fed GM corn. These are genes known to control protein synthesis and modification, cell signaling, cholesterol synthesis, and insulin regulation. Studies also show intestinal damage in animals fed GM foods, including proliferative cell growth and disruption of the intestinal immune system."

According to Jeffrey Smith, a leading national expert on the dangers of genetically modified organisms (GMOs) and the author of *Seeds of Deception: Exposing Industry and Government Lies About the Safety of the Genetically Engineered Foods You're Eating*, explained in a recent interview how most GMOs are "herbicide tolerant" and therefore have high amounts of herbicides in the food they produce. Smith stated, "Roundup (an herbicide used in GM foods) is directly toxic, linked with cancer, birth defects, endocrine disruption (aka hormonal imbalances), Parkinson's, and other diseases. A study released last month showed that rats fed Roundup in their drinking water at levels considered safe suffered massive tumors, premature death, and organ damage. Other lab animals showed severe reproductive failures, such as sterility, smaller and fewer offspring, infertile offspring, huge infant mortality, and even hair growing in the mouths of hamsters."

That's a lot of information, but basically these statements are saying that dozens of animal studies conducted over the last 10 years have shown a correlation between the ingesting of GM foods and immune system issues (such as the ones that activate autoimmunity), fertility issues, accelerated aging (such as the kind that happens in POA), insulin regulation issues (such as what happens in type 1 diabetes and PCOS), premature death, cancer, birth defects, and altered genetic expression (meaning these foods are affecting our epigenetics).

Avoid *all* GM foods.

Gluten-Free Products and Corn

Many gluten-free products contain corn. The corn found in many processed and packaged foods is usually the GM kind, as corn is one of the top GM food in the United States. (right next to soy). So if you're buying a product made from corn, be sure it is made from organic corn (as organic corn is not GM), and avoid anything containing high fructose corn syrup because it is toxic and not fertility friendly.

No Soy

Soy products, organic or not, are so overly processed that they are actually indigestible, toxic, and are a potent source of xenoestrogens, aka plant hormones, that can have a remarkably strong effect on the hormones within your body, namely the hormones that maintain your fertility. There is a lot of science out there on how soy is a hormonal disruptor. Just to highlight a couple: *The American Journal of Clinical Nutrition* published a study that showed that after women ate 60 grams of soy protein per day for 30 days, their menstrual cycle changed, resulting in skipped ovulations and irregular menstruation for three months following the cessation of eating soy protein, and *The American Nutrition Association* released a thorough review on the current available scientific literature that shows soy to be a hormonally disruptive antinutrient. Based on this research, I strongly urge you to avoid all soy and soy-based products.

Upwards of 70% of all packaged foods (even the ones in health food stores) contain soy and soy derivatives, so be sure to read your labels and avoid foods with any of the following ingredients:

Soy oil	Soy protein isolate	Hydrolyzed vegetable protein
Soy flour	Vegetable oil (this is usually soy oil)	
Textured vegetable protein (TVP)		Soy yogurt
	Soy milk	Soy cheese
Tofu	Hydrolyzed soy protein	

No Added Sugars

Basically, when you eat a food with an "added sugar," *even if it's natural and organic*, it causes your blood sugar levels to spike, which in turn causes your body to release insulin to try and regulate and balance your now high blood sugar level (think PCOS and type 1 diabetes). This is a normal process. When added sugars are consumed day in and day out, this can create what is called insulin resistance, where your body no longer responds to the insulin being released. This insulin resistance causes hormonal imbalances affecting important fertility hormones and can lead to infertility. Scientists at Harvard have shown that following a low-sugar diet that limits consumption of refined sugars may improve fertility and pregnancy outcome.

So read your labels and skip the added sugar! Some common names for added sugar include the following:

Agave nectar	Brown sugar	Cane crystals
Cane sugar	Corn sweetener	Corn syrup
Crystalline fructose	Dextrose	Evaporated cane juice
Fructose	Glucose	Fruit juice concentrates
Lactose	Invert sugar	High-fructose corn syrup
Maltose	Malt syrup	Raw sugar
Sucrose	Syrup	

No Pesticides

This diet is all about organic and pesticide-free foods (and non-GM) foods. Certain pesticides have been linked to reproductive disorders. In 2013, the journal *Obstetrics and Gynecology* published a paper stating, "Patient exposure to toxic environmental chemicals [i.e., pesticides] and other stressors is ubiquitous, and preconception and prenatal exposure to toxic environmental agents can have a profound and lasting effect on reproductive health across the life course." Said another way: exposure to pesticides and environmental toxins not only affects your fertility but the fertility of your future children. So, on the *Yes, You Can Get Pregnant* diet, there are *no* pesticides.

However, to make it easier on you, not all fruits and vegetables need to be purchased organic. Luckily for us, we have the Environmental Working Group (www.ewg.org/foodnews) doing a ton of work on the consumer's behalf to determine which foods are most important for us to buy organic. Here is their current "dirty dozen plus" list, the 12 fruits and vegetables that carry the highest pesticide loads and therefore should be purchased organic, and two "plus" crops, domestically grown summer squash and leafy greens, specifically kale and collards. These "plus" crops did not meet traditional "dirty dozen" criteria but were commonly contaminated with pesticides exceptionally toxic to the nervous system (I denoted these with a "+"). The EWG updates this list yearly:

Apples	Celery	Strawberries
Peaches	Spinach	Nectarines (imported)
Grapes	Sweet bell peppers	Potatoes
Cucumbers	Cherry tomatoes	Hot peppers
Kale/collard greens+	Summer squash+	

No Artificial Sweeteners

These substances are chemically derived and have been scientifically shown to have toxic effects on our bodies. Since these foodstuffs are chemicals and *not* food, I advise you to avoid them.

Common names for artificial sweeteners that you need to avoid include the following:

Nutrasweet	Aspartame	Cyclamate
Canderel	AminoSweet	Maltitol
Mannitol	Saccharin	Sorbitol
Xylitol	Sunette	Equal

Okay, to sum up: The Six Big No's are anything but fertility enhancing. These foodstuffs are doing scientifically proven, measurable harm to your health and your ability to get pregnant, so you absolutely need to avoid them. Now, let's talk about the foods you *can* eat.

> For those of you nonflesh eating ladies, I have made this guide somewhat flexible so that you can choose other healthy protein options, although I do want to encourage you to try your best to eat, at the very least, eggs and fish.

The Three Big Yes's

My recommended get-pregnant diet is very carnivorous as in TOM we believe there is no better Qi-rich, life-cultivating, nutrient-dense food out there than one that comes from a humanely raised, free-roaming, organic grazing animal source. And as I mentioned earlier in this chapter: the latest Western scientific research supports a protein-rich diet for fertility. Of course, we can get good amounts of protein from nuts and beans (and this diet recommends those foods as well), but animal products offer the most complete and digestible source of protein. Assume that everything on this list is organic, except for the foods that I just mentioned as not needing to be, and that all animal products are organic, pasture-raised, and grass-fed. As well, getting locally grown and in-season food is a major plus.

1. Animal protein
2. Fat
3. Fruits and vegetables

Eat Animal Protein

Don't be afraid of animal protein. These foods are rich in hormone-balancing essential nutrients such as iron, B vitamins, and saturated fats, which make them great for improving your egg quality and your overall fertility. Don't be afraid of saturated fats, they are loaded with fat-soluble fertility-enhancing vitamins such as A, K, and D (visit www.YesICanGetPregnant.com for more information on the top 10 fertility-enhancing nutrients). As well, saturated fats found in animal protein keep your blood sugar even, your energy high, and they will not give you high cholesterol. Keep in mind, a serving of meat or fish is about three to four ounces, or the surface area of your palm.

Healthy Fats You Should Cook With

Healthy fats play a critical role in your body—they enhance nutrient absorption and boost immune function as well as help your body make essential fatty acids (EFAs) and provide a rich source of fat-soluble vitamins, all of which is imperative to getting pregnant.

Any time I mention using a healthy fat, I am talking about one of the following:

- Olive oil (extra virgin and cold pressed)
- Coconut oil (extra virgin, raw, and cold-pressed)
- Butter (pastured)
- Ghee (from pastured cows)
- Sesame oil (extra virgin and cold pressed)

Margarine, canola oil, or any refined and chemically extracted vegetable oil (like corn or soy) are *not* healthy fats. These substances are processed and far from healthy, so steer clear of them!

- *Eggs* (pasture-fed organic eggs): *eat 8 to 12 per week.* Consume with the yolk. Egg yolks from pastured hens are deeply nutrient-dense—rich in fertility-boosting omega-3 fatty acids, vitamins A and E, and choline. Soft-boil, hard-boil, or pan-fry using a healthy fat (see the healthy fat box above).
- *Meat* (grass-fed, organic): *eat four to six servings per week.* Consume lean meat such as lamb, venison, grass-fed beef, buffalo,

pork, and turkey. Eat as lean as possible. Grass-fed beef is the only beef you should eat. Pan sear, grill, or broil.

> Visit www.YesICanGetPregnant.com for information on where to buy top-quality grass-fed meat.

- *Liver* (from a small fish or animal; cod, chicken, and lamb are the best sources): *eat one serving of 3 to 4 ounces per week.* Liver? Yes, liver. Liver is one of the best antioxidant, anti-aging, fertility-boosting foods that exist. It is a rich source of folate, vitamin B12, pantothenic acid, riboflavin, inositol, niacin, selenium, and vitamin A. A single 3.5-ounce portion of pan-fried chicken livers contains three times as much folate as an equivalent serving of raw spinach.

> Visit www.YesICanGetPregnant.com for the best places to buy liver.
>
> **Can't imagine yourself eating liver every week?**
>
> Take it in pill form. I take two liver pills each day, which is the equivalent of 3.5 ounces of liver per week. Don't skip on the liver as I feel this is one of the *most important* fertility-enhancing foods you can eat.
>   My *only* recommended brand is Dr Ron's, which you can purchase at www.DRRons.com or at www.YesICanGetPregnant.com.

- *Chicken* (pasture-fed, free-range, organic): *eat one to two servings per week.* Chicken contains arachidonic acid, which is an extremely inflammatory substance and can aggravate hormonal imbalances, so when eating animal protein, eat less chicken and more meat. Grill, bake, or cook on your stovetop using a healthy fat.
- *Homemade bone broth: drink 8 ounces three to five times per week.* Homemade bone broths are rich in calcium, magnesium,

phosphorus, glucosamine, and chondroitin and, most importantly, bone broths are rich in gelatin. Gelatin is a phenomenal source of fertility-enhancing protein, antioxidants, and amino acids. From a TOM perspective the gelatin in homemade bone broth provides your body with the essence it needs to engender health, longevity, and fertility. I strongly urge you to eat bone broth regularly; however, you can also take one tablespoon per day of a gelatin supplement as a great protein source that will amp up your fertility.

Boxed or canned broths and stocks, organic or not, are watered down stocks that pale in comparison to the nutrient density and flavor of homemade bone broths. Make your own essence-building bone broths by following the recipes on pages 193–196), the difference is immeasurable.

Or, visit www.YesICanGetPregnant.com to order your gelatin. I recommend Great Lakes or Pure Encapsulations brands.

- *Fish* (including deep-sea cold water fish, wild caught seafood, and shellfish): *eat 6 to 10 servings per week*. Fish, such as salmon, sardines, halibut, mackerel, oysters, clams, and cod are rich in omega-3 fatty acids, DHA and EPA, vitamins D and B12, as well as zinc. Broil, steam, or grill using a healthy fat. There are other great fish options depending on the region of the country you live in; check out Monterey Bay Aquarium's Seafood Watch (www.montereybayaquarium.org/cr/cr_seafoodwatch/download .aspx) for up-to-date info in your area.
- *Fish roe: eat 1 ounce one to two times per week.* Traditionally, fish roe has been known as a sacred food for pregnancy and lactation and it is a powerfully rich super food, with a high ratio of omega-3 to omega-6 fatty acids that aids in fertility for both men and women. Fish roe goes by a few names: caviar, tobiko (flying fish roe), and ikura (salmon roe). I prefer tobiko because the eggs are tiny and don't taste too fishy.

Visit www.YesICanGetPregnant.com for information on the best places to buy fish roe.

Full-fat dairy (organic, preferably pasture-fed and nonhomogenized): eat 4 ounces two times per week. (Don't eat dairy if you have autoimmune thyroid disease or a dairy allergy. Also, see chapter 10 for other instances where it may not be best for you to eat dairy.)

What if you have a dairy allergy?

Good substitutes for dairy are coconut products such as coconut milk, coconut oil, and coconut ghee.

As always, when purchasing any product: be sure to read the label and avoid any processed or artificial ingredients.

- *Butter: eat four tablespoons per week.* Pasture-fed full-fat butter produced from cows grazing on rapidly growing green grasses was historically considered an imperative food for fertility. This superbly nutrient-dense food is a potent source of fat-soluble vitamins A and K2, both of which positively influence reproductive health.

Protein substitutions:

2 eggs = 13 grams of protein
1 chicken sausage link = 13 grams of protein
3.5 ounces smoked salmon = 18 grams of protein
1 cup of hummus = 12 grams of protein
1 cup of Greek yogurt = 15 grams of protein
1 cup of cooked quinoa = 8 grams of protein
1 cup of coconut milk = 6 grams of protein

A good goal is to get about 25% of your daily caloric intake from protein. But don't overdo it. To figure out how much protein is too much for you, multiply your body weight in pounds by 0.7 (or body weight in kilograms by 1.5). Don't exceed that amount of grams of protein per day. For example, if you weigh 130 pounds, multiply 130 × 0.7= 91; so don't exceed 91 grams of protein per day.

Eat Healthy Fats from Oils, Nuts and Seeds

These foods are rich in antioxidants, phytonutrients, and omega fatty acids that are imperative to optimal health and fertility.

- *Organic oils: consume one to two tablespoons per day.* Extra virgin olive oil, coconut oil, and raw sesame oil (not toasted) are all great for you and rich in EFAs. These oils should be organic and cold pressed. *Avoid all other oils.* Olive oil, coconut oil, and sesame oil should be the only oils you use.

Beware: Cooking with Olive Oil and Sesame Oil

Olive oil is great for dressing salads and for cooking fish, but when it comes to cooking other foods (that require a high temperature to cook) olive oil isn't the best choice. At high temperatures (more than a medium flame or over 250 degrees Fahrenheit) olive oil (like flax seed oil) goes rancid, offers us no nutritional value, and can be harmful to your health. So, only use olive oil as an uncooked dressing or for cooking fish or chicken.

A good rule of thumb: if you're cooking with more than a medium flame on the stovetop: *don't* use olive oil or sesame oil. Use coconut oil, butter, or ghee instead.

- *Organic nuts and seeds: eat two tablespoons per day.* Nuts and seeds, such as flax seeds (grind them yourself, do not use flaxseed oil, only the seeds), almonds, cashews, walnuts, brazil nuts, filberts, sunflower seeds, sesame seeds, and pumpkin seeds are a great source of healthy fats, omega fatty acids, and provide an amazing energy boost during the day.

What if I have a nut or seed allergy?

Double up on your daily intake of the organic oils!

Eat Fruits and Vegetables

Fruits are a great source of vitamins, minerals, fiber, and antioxidants; however, they are typically high in sugar. And any food with a high sugar content, even if it's natural sugar, needs to be eaten in moderation. Eating too much sugar can cause insulin resistance and be hormonally disruptive. I want you to mainly indulge in fruits with the lowest amount of sugar and then once in a while have some really sweet fruit. Of course, it's ideal to eat fruits that are in season for your region.

- *Eat six to eight servings per week of a low-sugared fruit*: melons, berries, grapefruit, and avocado. Yes, that's any melon and any berry.
- *Eat only two to four servings per week of moderate to high sugared fruits*: apples, pears, plums, peaches, citrus (all others besides grapefruit), bananas, mangoes, pineapples, and fresh figs.
- *Dried fruits* are very high in sugar and should be consumed very sparingly—no more than once every two weeks.
- *100% pure juices, not from concentrate. You can have 4 ounces per day* pure cranberry or pomegranate juice as these two fruit juices are great for cleansing the liver. Because they are so tart, it is smart to dilute these juices with water: one-third juice to two-thirds water.

You should have one serving of a vegetable with each meal, that's *three to five servings per day!* A serving size for vegetables is 4 ounces or a half-cup. Green vegetables are particularly good at cleansing the liver, regulating PMS, and clearing up your skin (see list on following page). Prepare by steaming, sautéing, or roasting them in one of my recommended healthy fats. Once or twice a week, you can also make a fresh vegetable juice and drink your veggies. When you cook your vegetables, be sure you make them al dente, which means "to the tooth," that is, slightly undercooked; overcooked vegetables lose most of their nutrients.

Juicing and Your Fertility

Juicing has become very popular these days, and although it's a great way to get all of your veggies in, I want you to limit yourself to two to three fresh-pressed, organic juices per week. These juices are raw, and, from a TOM perspective, too cold for your child's palace. Also, science has shown that consuming large amounts of raw spinach and kale can inhibit your thyroid function, and this will impair fertility. If you have a diagnosed thyroid condition, I recommend you avoid consuming raw spinach, kale, and any other cruciferous vegetable. Rather, cook them and enjoy!

Some of My Favorite Fertility-Enhancing Veggies

- Leafy greens: Lettuce, spinach, kale, chard, collards, watercress, and kelp.
- Cruciferous veggies: Broccoli, Brussels sprouts, cabbage, cauliflower, and bok choy and garlic (these last two are a great source of anti-aging antioxidants).

> Eat two or more servings of cooked leafy greens and cruciferous vegetables *daily*!
>
> These vegetables contain a substance called indole-3-carbinol (I3C) which has been shown to block the production of toxic estrogens that cause diseases such as endometriosis, fibrocystic breasts, infertility, breast cancer, ovarian cancer, uterine cancer, and cervical dysplasia.
>
> Hint: An easy way to get at least one serving of greens per day is to take a greens superfood supplement daily. My favorite brands are Mega Foods, Garden of Life, or Pure Synergy.

- Onion
- Root veggies: Carrots, beets, squash, pumpkin, turnips, and parsnips. These veggies are rich in fertility–goodness boosting antioxidants, fiber, and nutrients (like folic acid and beta-carotene) that help balance our hormones.
- Mushrooms: Maitake, shiitake, ganoderma (lingzhi), reishi, and wood ear (aka black mushrooms). These specific mushrooms enhance the immune system, fight off cancer, and boost fertility.
- Legumes: Lentils, split peas, green beans, and garbanzo, pinto, and lima beans. These foods are loaded with fiber and minerals such as magnesium that help ease menstrual cramps. When it comes to eating beans, they *must* be prepared properly so that you can digest them, otherwise they do more harm than good to your digestive system. Prepare beans by soaking them before you cook them, as this helps break down the naturally occurring sugars in them. It's these sugars that make beans hard to digest

and give you gas. So soak your beans for six to eight hours (or overnight) before cooking. In a large saucepan, soak the beans in three times as much water as beans, add one tablespoon of lemon juice or one teaspoon of apple cider vinegar. If there's no time for a six-hour soak—no worries—you can quick-soak. Cover beans with water, bring to a boil, then turn off the heat and let sit for an hour or two. To make beans most digestible, always drain the soaking liquid and cook in fresh water.

- Sweet potatoes and yams: These foods are loaded with antioxidants and hormone-balancing vitamins. Eat at least one per week. To reduce the sugar load of these "starchy" veggies, be sure to eat them with a good fat, such as olive oil or organic butter.

Other *Yes, You Can Get Pregnant* Dietary Recommendations

Fermented Foods: One to Two Tablespoons per Day

Eating fermented foods such as sauerkraut, kimchi, pickled ginger, and kombucha is an incredibly healthy and traditional dietary practice. These foods supply your digestive system with good bacteria that are essential to breaking down the food you eat and assimilating the nutrients from that food.

Healthy, Organic Sweeteners: One to Two Teaspoons per Day

Healthy organic sweeteners can be consumed very moderately, including: maple syrup, organic and unsulfured blackstrap molasses, malt syrup, raw honey, brown sugar in the raw, and stevia can be used to sweeten things.

Limited quantities allowed of the following:

- *Alcohol*: If you are actively trying to get pregnant and want a drink, have purified alcohols such as top-shelf vodkas, scotches, whiskeys, and gins. Otherwise, avoid alcohol (or have it in strict moderation) if you think you could be pregnant.
- *Caffeine*: Coffee or teas should always be organic. Limit yourself to one cup of organic tea or coffee per day, or less than 100 mg of caffeine per day.

Fertility-Rejuvenating Nutritional Supplements

I'm not a huge fan of over-supplementation, but I am a fan of supplementing with certain nutrients we can't get from our diets. First and foremost, I believe that we should be able to get most of our nutrients from the foods we eat (especially when eating a diet like I just mapped out for you). However, with the current state of our precious American soil, organic or not, our foods aren't nearly as nutritious as they once were. For instance, in 1960 a plate full of food (meat, potatoes, and veggies) gave a person all the nutrients needed for that day. In today's world, with the state of our soil and the amount of pesticides and chemicals used on our foods, you would need to eat an entire wheelbarrow full of that same food to get all the nutrients you'd need for the day.

Bottom line: you need to supplement certain nutrients, especially if you are trying to conceive.

But this need for supplementation brings us to a whole new issue. How nutritiously sound are the vitamins we buy, and where do they come from? The 2006 *Physician's Desk Reference* states that only 8% to 15% of any synthesized nutritional supplement (i.e., those made in a laboratory) is actually absorbable by the human body. What this means is that vitamins that are not made from whole food sources are a complete waste of your money. Unfortunately, most of the vitamins on the market are made in laboratories where individual nutrients are created and then packed into nice little capsules for you to swallow. The problem here is that substances such as vitamin A or B6 do not exist in nature all by themselves. Vitamins coexist with other vitamins and phytonutrients. In order for the human body to assimilate these vitamins and use them to optimize bodily functions, they need to present themselves to us with their other vitamin and phytonutrient friends. So synthetic vitamins, although made with the best intentions, actually offer us no nutritional value and are a complete waste of our money.

Whole food–based vitamins are the way to go. Not whole food as in the store, whole food as in whole food, the way it occurs in nature. These vitamins deliver nutrients with their vitamin and phytonutrient friends so that we can absorb them and utilize them for all they're worth.

There are some really good companies out there making some highly absorbable vitamins. The following is a list of my currently recommended brands (keep in mind though that companies change manufacturing practices and ingredients from time to time, so always read labels.) Some of my favorite brands are:

- Garden Of Life
- Dr. Ron's
- MegaFoods
- Pure Synergy Company

You can purchase many of these brands of fertility-enhancing supplements on my website, www.YesICanGetPregnant.com.

Again, I don't over-recommend supplements. I think we should do our best to get our nutrients from our foods. I do, however, urge most everyone to take the following three supplements to assist them in achieving optimal health and fertility:

1. *Cod Liver Oil: one tablespoon per day.* I recommend cod liver oil over any other form of fish oil or omega-3 supplements since cod liver oil is by far the richest source of omega-3 EFAs. These EFAs play an important role in helping our bodies produce and regulate hormones, manage inflammation, and maintain a high functioning brain and nervous system. Omega-3 EFAs are commonly found in cold-water fish, flaxseeds, walnuts, legumes, nuts, and green leafy vegetables (and I want you to eat plenty of such omega-3–rich foods). However, since the typical American diet contains more omega-6 EFAs (found in foods like grains, plant-based oils, eggs, and poultry) than omega-3's, and a body in optimal health should have equal amounts, the key is to supplement with omega-3.

In addition, cod liver oil is a great source of vitamins A and D. Vitamin A helps your eyes adjust to light changes and keeps your eyes and skin hydrated, and vitamin D is essential for maintaining healthy bones and hormonal balance. Purchase this in capsule form or oil form. If you experience loose bowel movements after taking it, cut the dosage by half. The best, high-quality, mercury-free, *happy-fish* brands I recommend are:

○ *In store:* Garden Of Life regular-dose cod liver oil or Carlson's cod liver oil.

○ *Online:* Dr. Ron's high-vitamin old-fashioned blue ice pure cod liver oil (www.drrons.com) and Green Pastures blue ice, high-vitamin cod liver oil (www.greenpasture.org).

Vitamin D and Your Fertility

A deficiency in vitamin D can affect your ability to get pregnant and remain pregnant. Get your vitamin D levels checked by your doctor. Ideal vitamin D levels should be around 50 ng/ml. If your vitamin D levels are under 50 ng/ml, I recommend supplementing with 5,000 IU's of liquid vitamin D3 daily. My preferred brand is Pure Encapsulations.

---

2. *Green Superfood or Spirulina, one to two teaspoons per day or 6 to 10 grams per day.* Spirulina is a freshwater blue-green algae that's nearly three and one-half *billion* years old; it's a tremen-dously rich source of protein, EFAs, and vitamins such as B1, B2, B3, B6, B9, C, D, and E.
Bottom line: Spirulina is full of age-fighting, fertility-enhancing, antioxidants and it boosts your immune system.
   Spirulina comes in tablet, capsule, or powder form. Whichever brand you decide to get, take it as directed on the bottle. My all-time favorite, top-notch brands of spirulina are:

○ *In store:* Nutrex Hawaiian Organic Spirulina or Garden Of Life perfect food (take as directed).

○ *Online:* Pure Synergy Superfoods (take as directed) (www. thesynergycompany.com/v/pure_synergy.html)

3. *Probiotics:* The word probiotic means "for life." Probiotics are the good bacteria found in your digestive tract. Taking a probiotic supplement helps to maintain the natural balance of good and bad bacteria in your body, improves your digestion, and boosts your immune system. I'm sure you've heard of probiotics before—they're often touted as natural components of certain foods like Dannon's Activia yogurt. Like all nutritional supplements, probiotics come in all shapes and sizes and some forms are not worth your time or money. The key thing about ingesting a probiotic is that it needs to survive the harsh acidity in your stomach and make it to your small intestine so that it can actually give you some of its benefits. Eating foods enriched with a probiotic is pointless because they will get digested in the stomach and you won't get any benefit (not to mention you'd have to eat 10 yogurts to get the amount of probiotic found in one capsule). With that said, here are the brands of probiotics I recommend:

   ○ *In store:* Culturelle or Mega Foods (take one capsule per day)

Your Daily Dose of Fertility-Enhancing Supplements

Take these each day on a full stomach (except for probiotics—take them about 30 minutes before you eat):

- One tablespoon (or eight capsules) of fermented cod liver oil
- Six Pure Synergy Superfood (Spirulina) pills or one to two teaspoons of the powder
- One probiotic capsule

Now, that I've told you what to eat (and which supplements to take) to build your Qi, essence, and improve your egg quality, we need to also talk about what you are putting on your skin in the form of any of your beauty and body products. If you recall, the source of Qi in our body comes from:

1. The foods we eat
2. The air we breathe

What is meant by "the air we breathe" is not just that the quality of the air you are breathing should be fresh, clean, and nontoxic (and that you should be getting out into nature on a regular basis), but in addition, the body and beauty products you are putting on your skin also need to be nontoxic. The skin is our body's largest organ and it literally breathes in all of the products you put on it. With that said, turn the page and read about the importance of steering clear of environmental toxins in your body and beauty products.

6
Steering Clear of Environmental Toxins

The truth is, your personal care and household products contain endocrine-disrupting chemicals (EDCs) and they are messing with your fertility. According to the World Health Organization (WHO) website, EDCs are: mostly man-made chemicals found in various materials such as pesticides, metals, additives or contaminants in food, and personal care products. EDCs have been suspected to be associated with altered reproductive function in males and females, increased incidence of breast cancer, abnormal growth patterns and neurodevelopmental delays in children, and changes in immune function.

So, what does this mean to you?

Not only are nonorganic, pesticide-ridden foods compromising your fertility-rejuvenating process, but likely, the household and personal care beauty and body products that you are using are also negatively affecting your fertility.

When it comes to the beauty and body products you put on your skin, you must realize this: the skin is the largest organ and what you put on your skin seeps into your bloodstream and can affect how your body functions. Most importantly, the toxic EDCs found in commercial beauty products are causing your hormones to be out of whack, which in turn is causing your reproductive system to be out of whack.

It doesn't stop there. There are other serious environment-disrupting chemicals in things such as the products you use to clean your house, water bottles, food storage containers, and canned foods that can seriously affect your hormones and your fertility.

In September 2013, the American College of Obstetricians and Gynecologists (ACOG) and the American Society of Reproductive Medicine (ASRM) collaborated on the following statement: "Prenatal exposure to certain chemicals has been documented to increase the risk of cancer in childhood; adult male exposure to pesticides is linked to altered semen quality, sterility, and prostate cancer; and postnatal exposure to some pesticides can interfere with all developmental stages of repro-ductive function in adult females, including puberty, menstruation and ovulation, fertility and fecundity, and menopause."

In 2010, the journal *Frontiers in Neuroendocrinology* published a paper on EDCs and their effect on female reproduction. Here's an astonishing quote from the paper:

> The overall fertility rate of women aged 15–44 years in the United States dropped 44% between 1960 and 2002. Lifestyle choices may have been a major contributor of this decline as this study included all women in this age group. However, according to the data from the *National Survey for Family Growth*, the "impaired fertility rate" was increased from 11% to 15% between 1982 and 2002. Furthermore, the incidence of female reproductive disorders such as early puberty, irregular menstrual cycles, endometriosis, premature ovarian failure, and polycystic ovarian disorder is increasing in parallel with the increasing number of EDCs in the environment.

Basically, what the above statement translates to is: the endo-crine disruptors in our environment are causing an increase in female reproductive disorders and decreased fertility. Another research paper published in 2009 by the journal *Endocrine Reviews* con-cluded: "There is an association between potential exposure to other EDCs, such as bisphenol-A (BPA) and genistein (an isoflavone found in soybeans and soy products) and female reproductive problems." Levels of BPA in blood are associated with a variety of conditions in women including endometrial hyperplasia, recurrent miscarriages, sterility, and polycystic ovary syndrome (PCOS). Although BPA and genistein are not often found in beauty or body products, BPA is often in the containers they come in. And, genistein is soy-derived and can be found in food products as well as some body and beauty products (and from the nutrition information I just gave you, you know to avoid soy and soy products at all costs; this includes body and beauty products that contain soy).

> One of my favorite websites is the Environmental Working Groups Skin Deep Cosmetic Database (www.ewg.org/skindeep/). Here you can check the toxic load of your beauty products and find less toxic ones to replace them.

So if I'm telling you to avoid pesticides and toxic chemicals in your foods, I need to tell you to avoid them in your beauty and body products as well as in your household products, water bottles, and food storage containers. This means not just your makeup, but also your lotions, your deodorant, your toothpaste, your nail polish, your shampoo, your hair products. (Don't worry, I have a list of Aimee Approved beauty and body products that you can confidently use on page 191).

Bottom line: all of the household and personal care products you use must be free of toxic chemicals as these products could be the cause of your fertility challenges. Even if they're not the cause, they are not helping your situation.

In order to truly rejuvenate your fertility, you—hands down, no joke—must avoid the following 15 ingredients (the same way you must avoid gluten, soy, and added sugar):

1. *BPA:* This chemical is produced in large quantities for use primarily in the production of polycarbonate plastics and epoxy resins. Typically this is found in food and drink packaging like water and infant bottles, food storage containers, compact discs, impact-resistant safety equipment, and medical devices. Epoxy resins are used as lacquers to coat metal products such as food cans, bottle tops, and water supply

pipes. Some dental sealants and composites may also contribute to BPA exposure. Go for products packaged in glass or plastic and tin packaging that says BPA-free.

2. *Fragrance (aka artificial fragrance, synthetic fragrance, parfum, perfume):* These are used to make things smell good; however, these chemicals are scientifically proven hormonal disruptors. Look for products that are labeled "fragrance-free" and use essential oils to make things smell nice.

3. *Sulfates (sodium lauryl, sodium laureth sulfate (SLS), and sodium lauryl ether sulfate (SLES):* These are foaming agents and they make things lather up. They are usually found in toothpaste, shampoo, body washes, and soaps. These noxious substances are skin irritants, hormone disruptors, and carcinogenic. Also, be wary of labels that say "sodium lauryl sulfate (derived from coconut oil)" as they are trying to make it look as if it's natural and nontoxic, but the way they make coconut oil into SLS is through a highly chemical and toxin-producing process. Only buy products that are sulfate-free.

4. *Butylated hydroxyanisole (BHA) and butylated hydroxytoluene (BHT):* These two are common preservatives in moisturizers and makeup (and a lot of packaged food products). They are carcinogenic, cause thyroid problems, and have been shown to cause reproductive disorders.

5. *Parabens (methyl propyl butyl and ethyl):* We all know to avoid parabens, right? These guys are the worst. These EDCs are used to preserve products for longer shelf-life. They are also very disruptive to our hormones. Many believe parabens play a significant role in male *and* female infertility. Also, they have harmful implications in developing children and have been tied to the higher incidence of breast cancer. Avoid parabens at all costs, period.

6. *Polyethylene glycol (PEG, PEG-20):* This stuff is actually used in oven cleaner products as it is a powerful degreaser. You will find it in many baby wipes, skin cleansers and lotions, shaving cream, lip balm, and even contact solution and laxatives! PEG has been linked to kidney damage, leukemia, breast cancer, uterine cancer, and brain cancer; it is a cosmetic form of mineral oil

(refined crude oil) used in industrial antifreeze. People handling it are warned by the manufacturer to avoid skin contact and wear respirators and rubber gloves, yet this is a major ingredient in most moisturizers, skin creams, baby wipes, and sun screens? Why? It's cheap and gives the "glide" factor in body lotions—but it is, in fact, robbing moisture from lower layers of skin. Lanolin and collagen also clog pores and cause skin to age faster than if nothing was used. *Go PEG-free.*

7. *Phthalates (aka benzene, DEP, DBP, DEHP, and any word that has "phth" in it):* These noxious EDCs hit the headlines last year for being "gender benders." They are a family of industrial plasticizers already banned in the EU from being used in plastic toys, but are still used in hairsprays, top-selling perfumes, and nail varnishes. They can be absorbed through the skin, inhaled as fumes, and ingested from contaminated food or breastfeeding. Animal studies have shown they can damage the liver, kidneys, lungs, and reproductive system—especially developing testes. *Go phthalate-free.*

8. *Formaldehyde (aka DMDM hydantoin, diazolidinyl urea, imidazolidinyl urea, methenamine and quarternium-15):* When combined with water, this toxic gas is used as a disinfectant, fixative, germicide, and preservative in deodorants, liquid soaps, nail varnish, and shampoos. Also known as formalin, formal, and methyl aldehyde, it is a suspected human carcinogen and has caused lung cancer in rats. It can damage DNA; irritate the eyes, upper respiratory tract, and mucous membrane; and may cause asthma and headaches. It is banned in Japan and Sweden.

9. *Toluene:* A common solvent found in nail enamels, hair gels, hair spray, and perfumes. It is a neurotoxin and can damage the liver, disrupt the endocrine system, and cause asthma.

10. *Talc:* A known carcinogen that has been linked to an increased risk of ovarian cancer and general urinary tract disorders. So don't dust it on your baby's, or anyone else's, bottom!

11. *Oxybenzone (aka benzophenone, ethoxycinnamate, PABA):* This sunscreen chemical will not only disrupt your hormones but can damage DNA and lead to certain cancers.

12. *Diethanolamine (aka Tri and Mono, DEA, TEA, and MEA):* An EDC that is used in creamy and foaming products. This toxin is absorbed through skin and has been shown to be carcinogenic.

13. *Aluminum:* This is most commonly found in deodorants and has been linked to diseases such as Alzheimer's disease and breast cancer.

14. *Triclosan (aka 5-chloro-2-(2,4-dichlorophenoxy) phenol):* This anti-microbial/antibiotic agent is found in hand sanitizers, deodorants, toothpastes, vaginal washes, and mouthwashes. It has been found to negatively affect the thyroid, fertility, fetal development, and can lead to an increased risk of miscarriage.

15. *Petrolatum (aka mineral oil, petroleum):* A known carcinogen that is used to make products slick and moisture-rich. It's found in everything from hair spray to shampoo to mouth wash. Avoid it.

I'm sure this list is a lot to digest. So my general recommendation is to read labels of *all* products that come in contact with your skin or are used in your home and only put on your precious body or use in your home products with ingredients that don't sound like chemicals. My personal rule of thumb is, I don't put anything on my skin that I couldn't eat; I suggest you do the same. But beware that companies change ingredients regularly, so again, please, always read labels.

Keep in mind, there are definitely a lot of products out there that we can use and feel good about it, but just because something says "all natural" or "organic" doesn't always mean it's free of toxic chemicals. Add "read all labels of my body, beauty, and household products I come in contact with" to your to-do list for this week and start eliminating them from your life! Then, after you complete that

To learn more about good-for-you household and beauty products, including my own line of fertility-friendly skin care products, and a helpful handout to take with you when you go shopping for products, visit www.YesICanGetPregnant.com.

task, share this information with everyone you love as these EDCs are doing so much harm to us as a society, way beyond fertility problems.

Now that we have the diet and household and beauty product information, we are going to head into the last phase of your fertility rejuvenation lifestyle overhaul. The next chapter touches upon one of the most important aspects, and the least discussed, regarding our fertility challenges: your mental–emotional space. So drop your shoulders, open your heart, and get ready: we are going to dig into the emotional aspects of allowing yourself to become a mother.

7
Preparing Yourself Mentally and Emotionally

Now that you are armed with the first three pillars of the *Yes, You Can Get Pregnant* fertility rejuvenation way of life, I want you to tune into the natural rhythm of your fertile body and answer the following questions. Be honest.

Are you approaching getting pregnant like a work project for a job that feels beyond your innate capabilities?

Are you so tense over the topic of fertility rejuvenation that you're reading this book with your shoulders up to your ears?

Is every menstrual cycle a new opportunity for you to beat yourself up for not being pregnant?

Are you walking around, staring at every pregnant woman you see and feeling anger?

Do you think you are undeserving of having everything you want, especially pregnancy?

If you said yes to any of the above questions, we need to dig a little deeper into your mental–emotional state and how it's affecting your fertility (If you said no, keep reading anyway).

We have already talked about the importance of believing in your body and your fertility, but consider this: all this "work" you are doing to get pregnant may be working against you. For example, are you beating yourself up over all the things you *could* be doing but you're *not* doing? Are you reading this book and thinking, *Great, just one more thing I have to do to get pregnant while everyone just gets pregnant whenever they want?* The perception that rejuvenating your fertility is "work" that you don't want to do, but that you *have* to do, may be making this journey more difficult for you *and* that attitude is bad for your health and your immune system.

In fact, research published in the journal *Fertility and Sterility,* based on 151 women scheduled to undergo an IVF cycle, found that the chance of a live birth was 93% higher in women with the highest positive-affect score. Said another way, the positive women were 93% more likely to get pregnant than the negative women. In another study published in the same journal, researchers found that women with symptoms of depression were half as likely to conceive as women who were not depressed. This research is clear: positive, joyful, grateful women are more likely to get pregnant than women who are negative and doubtful. Yes, your mental attitude plays a significant role in your health and your fertility.

When you look at something and you think, *I don't think I'm capable of this* and then you prove yourself right; that's called a self-fulfilling prophecy and people do it all the time. I am encouraging you to avoid that pitfall with your fertility. Don't psyche yourself out. Don't go into this with the wrong mentality. Yes, meditating daily, changing your diet and your beauty products may put a few more things on your to-do list, however, these things are for the benefit of your health and the health of your future child.

I know that making the changes I recommend will most definitely improve your health, and the fertility will naturally come second to your overall better health. However, I want to make sure that you aren't approaching this book as another stress-inducing, full-time job that you think you might not be good at. Total fertility rejuvenation is about you forming such a strong belief in your body and its ability to be healthy and fertile that you are confidently moving forward and making changes with eagerness and excitement. This is not about you begrudgingly taking on the recommendations on these pages. I encourage you to dive in and eat organic because it tastes better, skip the gluten because you will feel less bloated when you don't eat it, and say your mantra loud and proud because it feels good. Do it for your essence, Qi, and blood, and let the fertility and the motherhood come to you. *Exercise your power to make changes in your health and believe that your fertility will thrive as an awesome consequence.*

Start witnessing the results of your enriched lifestyle in an improved menstrual cycle, better digestion, more restful sleep, a happier disposition, and then sit back and let the fertility flow to you. When, through lovingly and eagerly following the advice in this book, you achieve optimal health, your fertility will improve, and you will be in a better position of getting pregnant and becoming a mother. On the other hand, I can say for sure that if you are looking at all of this like it's hard work, you will be exhausted.

Your Self-Love Health Mission

Here's an idea: you should look at these adjustments to your lifestyle that will improve your fertility as a self-love health mission. Rather than looking at this as some intense must-do project that you're going to beat yourself up over if you don't do it, let's shift your attention. The same way we have shifted your focus to fertility and away from *my least favorite word*, I want you to shift your focus from this being work to this being your self-love health mission. It's this mission, when you embrace it, that will empower you with abundant health and fertility. Your self-love health mission will turn back your biological clock, keep your genes from shifting from a good place to a not so good one, and it will fill your child's palace with fertile essence, Qi, and blood. Your hair and skin will glow, you will feel lighter and clearer, you will be happier, and life will feel easier. Yes, the bottom line is to get pregnant, but I want to make sure you understand that when you are in optimal health, physically *and* emotionally, you will be fertile into your 40s. Health comes first, fertility second; a self-love health mission comes first, an ability to get pregnant is the result.

Doubtful? Ponder this: if you've done everything you believe you're *supposed to do* and you're still being hard on yourself because you're not yet pregnant, then what gives? I am suggesting that there is a deeper emotional component at work. Maybe all that frustration over how much work you *have to do* is actually harming your health. Maybe it's more than just eating to improve egg quality or turning off your electronics an hour before bed to get back in touch with nature. As I've said throughout this book, our health and our fertility are dependent not only on our physiology but also on our mental–emotional state. Sure, you can eat organic all you want, avoid toxic beauty products and become one with nature, but you need to also allow joy and confidence and a resolute belief in your body and its health to take root in your life. Likewise, I am here to encourage you to let go of the negative thoughts and stories that aren't serving you. My job is to remind you that not one of those negative emotions is good for you. They hurt your health and your fertility. Harboring pessimism and doubting your body and its fertility hurts your heart and your uterus and it chips away at your precious fertility-enhancing essence.

So we are now going to shift our focus: your fertility-rejuvenation journey is *not* work, it's a self-love health mission. Keep in mind: you are adopting these changes because you love yourself, because you know you deserve to feel better, because you believe in your ability to shift your health and your fertility.

> *It's time to repeat your new mantra:*
> *I have the power to change MY health and improve MY fertility.*

Yes, you do. You also have the ability to shift your perception: fertility rejuvenation feels good and you deserve to feel good. Period.

Allowing Yourself to Become a Mother

The mental–emotional component to your ability to conceive is extremely important. The art of allowing yourself to become a mother is just as important, if not more so, than eating organic and cutting out soy and gluten and repeating your mantra. Allowing yourself to become a mother is about softening to this process of fertility rejuvenation. It's about acceptance of where you are and being at peace with the fact that you are not yet pregnant. It's about being in a place of, *it's OK that I'm not pregnant yet, as I know I will be soon.*

In this section we are going to look into all the reasons you are excited about being a mother, why motherhood will add to your life, and why becoming pregnant and being a mother will feel so dang good. Additionally, we are going to learn to let go of all the reasons why you are being so hard on yourself, why you are holding onto *your beliefs about why* you don't have what you want. The first step to allowing yourself to become a mother is letting go.

Letting Go

The health and vitality of your organs, your child's palace included, is affected by the emotions that are running through your body. For the love of your fertility, it is now time to let go of the most common health and fertility-destroying emotions: fear, anger, and sorrow. I know, easier said than done. I also know those emotions need to be felt. Letting go is not about repressing emotions, as that is not healthy. However, harping on these emotions isn't productive either. Allowing these negative emotions to take up space in your life is preventing more positive ones from coming in. Most importantly, these negative emotions are severing healthy energy, essence, and spirit from flowing to your uterus, your child's palace, and that is preventing pregnancy from happening. Letting go is about surrendering, it is about being easy on yourself, it is about accepting where you are, and it is about believing that you are doing the best you can do and all that you desire is coming to you.

Before we can officially decide to let go, we need to identify what it is we are holding onto. What beliefs or resentments or situations are we gripping onto that are holding us back from motherhood? In Traditional Oriental Medicine (TOM) we recognize five different emotional states that, when experienced over prolonged periods of time, have a very detrimental effect on your health, your fertility, and the organs they are associated with:

- Fear (associated with the kidney)
- Anger (associated with the liver)
- Grief (associated with the lung)
- Excessive worry (associated with the spleen)
- Sorrow (associated with the heart)

Experiencing all of these emotions once in a while is normal and encouraged. It is when any one of these emotions is experienced over long periods of time, say six months or more, that they can become destructive to your health and to your fertility. In my practice, the most prominent emotions I see present in women longing to become mothers are anger, fear, and sorrow. Who wouldn't be pissed off, scared, and miserable about not being able to get what they want, especially when they are working so damn hard to get pregnant?

However, there is a point that I'd like to drive home: these emotional states tend to become accepted and tolerated by my patients (and their loved ones, friends, coworkers, and anyone else they come into contact with) who are dealing with infertility. This acceptance of negative emotions *worsens* your chances of getting pregnant.

Anger makes your whole body tense and defensive. It is by no means an emotion that helps you be receptive and welcoming to a baby, let alone your partner whom you need to have sex with to get pregnant. Anger is also the emotion of the liver, an organ in TOM that is one of the most important organs in regulating our hormonal system and making for a smooth menstruation. The liver longs to be at peace, to accept, to surrender, to go with the flow of life. When the liver is constantly angry and tense, your hormones are all out of whack, your menstrual cycle is likely irregular and filled with PMS, and getting pregnant is unlikely.

Fear is so destructive. Similar to excessive worry, fear makes you feel weak in the knees, nauseous, out of control. It can turn your heart black. Fear is the emotion of the kidneys, and as you know by now the kidneys are responsible for your essence. Essence is the crux of your fertility. The more you muddle in your fear, the more you chip away at your courage and confidence, the more you damage your essence, and the further you move away from motherhood.

Sorrow hurts your heart and severs its necessary connection to your child's palace. Sorrow and grief are related emotions and they both make you feel heavy and discouraged. When you hold onto sorrow you block joy and optimism and your spirit, your inner radiance, has no light. You literally look dark and dreary. And your health suffers.

So, how do you get through these emotions? How do you find a way to be kind to yourself the majority of the time? How do you learn to accept the fact that this is your challenge and you must remain optimistic and persevere?

Joy and gratitude are the antidotes to sorrow.
Acceptance and peace are the antidotes to anger.
Confidence and courage are the antidotes to fear.

I encourage you to find a way to bring joy and acceptance and confidence to your daily life. I am cheering for you to find the upside in your situation. I am eager for you to focus on the positive. I am optimistic that you will find peace in your life. I know some days it's hard. I know some days you just want to deck the next friend who tells you she's pregnant, or you want to take that negative pregnancy test and shove it into your doctor's eye, or just sit home and cry and feel sorry for yourself. That anger, fear, and sorrow makes sense. It does. But these emotions, when experienced on a regular basis, are seriously having a negative effect on your health and are impeding your chances of becoming pregnant.

Now let's get to the letting go.

The following page includes a list of the 10 most common fertility-limiting statements I hear women say. I'd like you to read each sentence out loud and tune into two areas of your body: your solar plexus (located in the center of your abdomen) and the center of your chest (located in the center of your breast bone). When you read each sentence, do you feel a reaction or a sensation in either part of your body? This tells us if you identify with and are holding onto a belief about the statement.

Take a few moments and sit quietly, tuning into your body and read each sentence out loud. For any sentence that resonates in either your chest or your solar plexus, make a check mark next to it. This is a stressful statement that you are somehow, someway, believing to be true, and it is affecting your fertility.

These are very big topics and I don't want to do them any disservice by speaking generally about them. However, in the confines of this book, we can't get super deep into such specific topics as the ones I listed above. But, we can do some work to aid you in identifying any repressed emotions you may have and then give you tools to use so you can allow yourself to let them go. Of course, some of you have some major traumatic experiences that you

(continued)

(continued)

> may or may not have sought psychological help for, and I always encourage using a psychotherapist, psychiatrist, or other mental health worker when needed. This work here is more general and really aimed at getting you to identify what you are holding onto that may be disallowing you to become the mother you long to be.

I have a fear that I won't be able to get pregnant.

I have a fear that I may not be a good mother.

I have fear about all the changes that motherhood/parenting will bring.

I have a fear that my partner won't be a good parent.

I am still sad over a past traumatic event (miscarriage, death of a loved one, loss of a significant relationship).

I am afraid to have a child that has something "wrong" with him/her.

I don't have much joy in my life and I am hoping motherhood will fix it.

Things never go right for me; that's why I can't get pregnant easily.

I am angry that every other mother has what I want.

I am angry about all the pressure being put upon me to get pregnant.

OK, take a deep breath. Those statements are deep and often bring up heavy emotions. That's the point here: I want the emotion to come up for you and then I encourage you to make a conscious decision to let it go.

Let's take another look at the statements you put a check mark next to. I want you to reread the statements and ask yourself, *is this statement really true?* Do I really, in my heart of hearts, believe it to be true?

Next, get out a pen and some paper and I want you to write out the stressful sentence that resonated the most in your chest or your solar plexus. Then, on the next line, I want you to write out five reasons why the stressful statement is *NOT* true.

For example:

Stressful statement: I have a fear that I won't be able to get pregnant.

This statement is not true because:

1. I have the power to improve my health and my fertility.
2. I believe in my body's ability to get pregnant.
3. I know other women who are my age who have gotten pregnant.
4. I have always seen myself becoming a mother.
5. I am going to get pregnant when the time is right.

Let's try another one:

Stressful statement: I don't have much joy in my life and I am hoping motherhood will fix it.

This statement is not true because:

1. My friendships bring me joy.
2. Taking trips with my partner brings me joy.
3. Being around my family brings me joy.
4. Taking steps to improve my health brings me joy.
5. Exercising brings me joy.

Now, you give it a try. I want you to refute those stressful statements that you're believing. Step outside yourself, and speak to yourself with love and optimism and cheer yourself out of believing the stressful statement that you wrote out (the one that resonated the most in your chest or solar plexus) and into believing the opposite is true.

Next, I want you to write five times:

"I give myself permission to let go of the statement,_____ (fill in the blank with the stressful statement you just wrote down). I choose to let this belief go because I am worthy of happiness. I choose to let this belief go and I allow myself to become a mother."

For example, if "fear that I won't be able to get pregnant" is your stressful statement, then it will look like this:

I give myself permission to let go of the fear that I won't be able to get pregnant. I choose to let this belief go because I am worthy of happiness. I choose to let this belief go and I allow myself to become a mother.

Write it out five times.

If more than one of the statements resonated with you, then do this exercise for each of them. Basically, you are working through letting go of fear, sorrow, and anger beliefs and replacing them with happiness, joy, and confidence beliefs. You can do this. Even if you don't think it is that important for you to do, I want you to muster up the courage to do this. Keep in mind that letting go of these negative beliefs will take more than just doing this exercise once; this is a process and will likely have to be worked through on a regular basis. So each day, take the time to tune into your body, be present, and recognize the emotional state you're in, and if it's anything other than joy, gratitude, peace, or confidence, then choose to surrender to it, accept it, and do the work to let go of it. This chapter will help you begin to shift from a negative belief place to a positive belief place. Starting the letting go process for you is extremely important so that you can make space for more joy, peace, and confidence in your life.

Theresa was a 29-year-old high school teacher who was referred to my practice by a mutual friend. She and her husband had been trying to get pregnant for 14 months. She read my first book, *Chill Out and Get Healthy* and was following the fertility diet recommendations she got from our mutual friend. She was doing "everything" and it wasn't working. She didn't want to see a fertility doctor, as she told me over e-mail: she wanted to get pregnant naturally or not at all.

When I did her initial intake I found that she was extremely heart blood and essence deficient (see chapter 10); she barely slept a solid night because her dreams were so vivid and anxiety-ridden. Her hair was thinning, she was losing weight for no reason, she had heart palpitations all day long. Her periods were getting shorter in cycle length and lighter in blood flow.

Based on the lifestyle and dietary recommendations she told me she was following, I couldn't make sense as to why her health was declining. I thought to myself, *this has to be emotionally based.* So I asked her about her dominant emotional state and she said, "I'm just not happy." She

(continued)

(*continued*)

started to cry and began to tell me how unhappy she was in her marriage, how scared she was to bring children into it because then she could "never get out," how much pressure her husband and her family were putting on her to get pregnant, and how utterly miserable she was.

By our fourth treatment, Theresa had moved out of her home with her husband and begun talks with a lawyer about divorce. On top of all that, she was sleeping better and slowly gaining back weight.

She just wasn't ready to get pregnant because she wasn't happy in her marriage.

She will get pregnant when, or if, she is ever ready.

Here's another exercise I want you to do: Find a quiet place, sit still in a comfortable position, tune into your body, and say the following words to yourself, one at a time:

Fear
Anger
Sorrow

How did they feel? What did you feel when you said each of these words? I want you to tune in and recognize how these words physically affected you and write down three descriptions for how you felt when you said each of those words. For example:

Fear. I felt:

1. *Tension in my neck*
2. *My heart race*
3. *A pit in my stomach*

Anger. I felt:

1. *Pissed off*
2. *My jaw clench*
3. *Like I wanted to run and scream*

Sorrow. I felt:

1. *Heavy*
2. *Like I wanted to cry*
3. Uncomfortable in my own skin

Next, do the same thing for the words:

Confidence
Peace
Joy

Aren't these much better feeling emotions? Don't you feel lighter when you say them? Here are some things you may have felt when you said those positive words to yourself:

Confidence. I felt:

1. *Like I was taller*
2. *Proud of who I am*
3. *Sure of my ability to prepare my child's palace*

Peace. I felt:

1. *My shoulders drop*
2. *At ease*
3. *Love for myself*

Joy. I felt:

1. *Light*
2. *A smile come over my face*
3. *Positive*

It is likely that getting a good feeling from those last three positive emotions was harder for you then you'd like to admit. That's totally normal. Later in this chapter, I have an exercise to help you remember what those feelings feel like.

Before we move on, I want you to give yourself permission to let go of any of those stressful statements and negative emotions. Let go. Set them free. Tell them you don't have space in your life for them anymore. Let your body house more hope and positivity and less negativity. Make the choice *right now* to have more confidence than fear, more joy than sorrow, and more peace than anger. A big part of allowing motherhood into your life is letting go of the beliefs that may be holding you back. This is where the part of you that knows she deserves to feel peace, joy, and confidence can flourish. I know that part of you exists. Let's allow that part of you out; let's let her find her place in this world; let's let her dance and smile and find joy.

> If you are doing these exercises and you just don't see joy coming into your life, or you have longstanding depression and anxiety issues, don't be afraid to ask for professional help. This book cannot replace the value of meeting with a trained professional.

Bringing More Joy, Confidence, and Peace into Your Life

Fertility and conception are dependent upon *joy* in your heart, *confidence* in your health and fertility, and *peace* with where you are currently in life. Inside of you is a woman who confidently welcomes joy and peace into her everyday life. Inside of you is a fertile goddess on a self-love health mission who is brimming with fertility.

> YOU have the power to change YOUR health and to improve YOUR fertility.

Shifting from the emotional places of fear, anger, and sorrow to confidence, peace, and joy *will* improve your fertility. I am going to show you the ways you can allow these emotional states—joy, confidence, and peace—to flourish in your life.

> Melissa came to me as a new patient with two concerns: jaw tension related to migraines and fertility. She was a 41-year-old high-powered executive who was chronically under a ton of stress. She worked nonstop. Her husband was the same way. They started trying to

(continued)

(continued)

get pregnant on their honeymoon, which was six months prior. The first time we met she came in with a migraine and she was a day late for her period. I treated the migraine and told her to go home and take a pregnancy test. She e-mailed the next day that she got her period right after the treatment, but her migraine was gone.

As with all of my fertility clients, Melissa began following my fertility rejuvenation protocol. Like most of my "type A, New York City" clients, Melissa took her fertility rejuvenating job very seriously. She did everything: daily mantras, food diary, no gluten, no sugar, liver pills, all of it. She would e-mail me spreadsheets of her food diary. As we worked together, all her health issues resolved: no more migraines, her period completely regulated itself, she lost weight, her hormonal acne cleared up, her energy improved, her sleep was restful, and her digestion was seamless. Everything was great. But she still wasn't pregnant.

So after three months of working together and the pressure building from her gynecologist to see a fertility doctor (Melissa did not want to see a fertility specialist, even though I also encouraged it), I openly asked her, "Do you think there is anything that you are holding onto emotionally that may be holding you back from getting pregnant? Because at this point, your body is ready, but I sense your heart is not." She thought about it and said, "Let me think about that and get back to you."

Two weeks passed and Melissa was in for her next appointment. During her intake I asked her if she had given any thought to my question. She closed her eyes, clenched her jaw, shook her head up and down and said, "Yes." I motioned for her to lie back on the treatment table, and as I touched her wrist to feel her pulse I asked, "Do you want to tell me?" She turned her head away from me and began to talk, "You know Max is seven years younger than me, right? Well, we dated for four years before he proposed to me. He made me wait. He would break up with me, then come back, then break up with me again. It was so dramatic. And then finally after some serious pressure

(continued)

(*continued*)

from his family, he proposed to me. The thing is, the whole time I kept reminding him of my age and that I didn't have much time to wait to get pregnant and I always wanted three kids...anyway, I've just been so damn angry with him for making me wait, and now I can't get pregnant." She started to sob. I stood there and let her cry. "I'm just so pissed at him. I do love, him but every time he tries to talk to me about how bad he wants kids I just want to deck him. I have wanted them for the last four years."

I walked to the other side of the table so I could make eye contact with her, "Melissa, you've got to talk to Max about this. You have to tell him how you feel. These repressed emotions are eating you up, likely hurting your marriage, and preventing you from getting pregnant. You're so livid with him that your body is probably rejecting his sperm every time you attempt to conceive." Melissa laughed and said, "You're probably right. I love him but he repulses me right now."

It turns out that all that anger was really holding Melissa back from what she wanted. She and Max eventually talked it through, she agreed to see a fertility specialist (who told her to keep trying naturally for another three months because everything looked good), and I recommended that every day she write down five reasons why she loved Max. Melissa got pregnant two months later. She and Max are now happy parents and are now pregnant with their second baby. Melissa got pregnant naturally, twice, first at 41 and again at 43. Anger was her fertility issue.

Again, this is a process, so be patient with yourself, and kind to yourself, too. I am now reminding you that *you have the power to change your health and your fertility*. You have the ability to stop believing these negative stories you are telling yourself just as you have the ability to choose joy. You have the ability to confidently and courageously embrace your self-love health mission. You have the ability to find peace with where you are in your life, on your new self-love health mission that will rectify your health and your fertility and free you of the emotional burdens that are holding you back from pregnancy.

If you think this part of the book doesn't apply to you, you're not alone, as most of my patients ignore this aspect of their fertility treatment. I often hear comments such as:

"Aimee, I'll find joy when I'm pregnant."

"I'll have confidence in my health when my body does what I want it to do."

"I'll be at peace with where I am when I have what I want."

No. This type of thinking does not work. It does not support your self-love health mission.

I am here to urge you to find joy *now*. Visualize joy. Remember a time when you were happy. Remember when you fell in love with your partner. Or when you got that promotion and you were on top of the world. Or when you confidently believed in your health and your fertility. Remember the time when all that you wanted you felt was within your reach and you courageously went after it. That's the place we need you to find. Whether you had it once and you lost it or you have never had it, I am here to guide you to the joyful, confident, and peaceful place where fertility and health reside. When you get to that place where you find joy in your "here and now" and joy in the knowing that one day soon you will become a mother, you will allow motherhood into your life. Alternatively, holding onto the negative emotions that I just guided you to let go of will disallow motherhood. Let me explain it one more time: You disallow motherhood when you get angry at every pregnant woman you see. You disallow motherhood when you have fear and anxiety over your ability to get pregnant. You disallow motherhood when you feel hopeless and sad and continue to talk about all the reasons why you are fertility challenged.

I'm not saying those moments aren't going to come up. In fact, those moments and feelings are normal and they are going to happen, and likely each day you will need to make the choice over again: joy over sorrow, peace over anger, confidence over fear. This is your work to do each and every day. Each time a negative thought comes up, combat it with a positive one. Joy allows motherhood. Gratitude allows motherhood. Being happy for others allows motherhood. Confidently and excitedly expecting to one day soon become a mother allows motherhood. Knowing in your heart of hearts that motherhood will come to you allows it. If you haven't been practicing that daily joy exercise from chapter 1, please start doing it. Focusing daily on the joy in your life *right now* is imperative.

> **Make a conscious choice to choose:**
>
> **Joy over sorrow**
> **Peace over anger**
> **Confidence over fear**

Let's get into some more tools that you can use daily to bring more joy, confidence, and peace into your life.

Get out your pen and paper again. Tune into the natural rhythm of your fertile body and take some time to think about what it will be like to be a mother. What will it feel like? What will it look like? Is your life set up for it right now? Are you and your partner ready to be parents? Are you excited about raising a child? These are big thoughts to contemplate, but I want you to ponder them and then I want you to come from a positive, knowing, *I will be a mother* place, and write down five to ten reasons why becoming a mother will be the best thing ever. For example:

1. Being a mother will be amazing to see the wonder in my child's eyes.
2. It will be so enriching to watch my child grow up.
3. I can't wait to see my child performing in his/her first school play.
4. Being a mother will teach me so much about myself.
5. People always say that your kids bring out the best in you and I am so excited to experience that.
6. It going to be so joyful to be a mother.
7. My child will be a daily inspiration to me.

OK, your turn. You can use some of the reasons I just wrote out or make your own list. Again, write this list from a positive, knowing, motherhood-will-happen-for-me place. After you've written down your five to ten reasons why becoming a mother will be the best thing ever, reread this list three times, out loud, and notice the happy, feel-good emotions that run through you when you believe that motherhood will be yours. Get out your pen and write them down right now; for example:

1. Joy
2. Excitement
3. Elation
4. Eagerness
5. Gratitude

Focus on those emotions. Find a way to feel them as often as you can. Staying in a state of optimism is not only uplifting to your spirit and your heart and your child's palace but it allows motherhood (and all the things you want in your life) to come to you. The allowing part of motherhood is knowing it will come to you and then opening up to allow it. Get to the excited *oh my goodness, it's going to happen soon* place, and own it.

Combat any of the negative, self-doubting, *I don't believe* thoughts with uplifting and hopeful thoughts, and by all means, believe in your mantra.

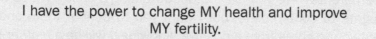

> I have the power to change MY health and improve MY fertility.

Know that a huge part of where this power comes from is your belief that you are fertile, that you will get pregnant, that you are where you're supposed to be and you are going to become a mother. You are on this self-love health mission for a reason: to better your health, to find more joy and peace and confidence in your life, and to allow fertility into your life.

Often, I say to patients, "Even if you spend 55% of your time in the believing place and 45% of your time in the disbelieving place, that's good enough." It really is. Ideally, we are in a joyous place more than 55% of our lives, but the key is to be more joyful than sorrowful, more at peace than angry, more confident than fearful. A great way to do this is to start telling a new story about your life.

Giving Birth to Your New Story

As one of my spiritual teachers taught me, "Your life is the story you tell yourself, so tell a good one." Basically, the story you tell of yourself can wind up defining you. It can wind up becoming your life. If you tell everyone about your fertility struggles, you become that person that everyone sees as the one who is struggling with fertility. Alternatively, you can tell a better story, a fertility-rejuvenated positive story, and you will shift your life in that direction. You can create your reality through recreating your story. In each moment we have the choice to see the situation the way we choose to see it. You can look around and focus on all the women who are experiencing "fertility challenges" *or* you can look around and see all the pregnant women and their abundant fertility. You can look at a pregnant woman and get angry, *or* you can look at her and feel joy for her and feel joy knowing that you too will be pregnant one day. You can change your diet and remove toxic beauty products from your life and moan about it, *or* you can make these lifestyle changes because you are on your self-love health mission and it feels good. You can talk to every person you know about your "fertility challenges," *or* you can decide to focus on all the fertility around you and know that you, too, are fertile.

How we see a situation, how we describe it, how we react to it is all entirely in our control. This is another part of that word "power" in your mantra: *I have the power to change MY health and improve MY fertility*. You have the power to choose how you feel and how you tell your story to yourself and to everyone else.

Tell me, what does your self-talk sound like? Is it something like, *I'm still not pregnant and everyone else is, I think I'll eat some worms?* Or, *I am nothing if I'm not a mother*. Or, is it something like, *Things never work out for me, so why should getting pregnant be any different?*

Stop right now. We are going to start telling a new story. Now.

From here on out: you are on a self-love health mission. You are fertile. You are going to be a mother. You are going to be an outstanding mother. You can see that positive pee-stick pregnancy test, you can see yourself brimming with pregnancy, you can see yourself holding your newborn baby, you can see yourself being a mother. Get out that pen and paper again and write out the following:

I no longer believe the negative thoughts about my fertility.
*I have joy in my life thanks to*_____
(fill in the blank with three, four, or five things that bring you joy in your daily life) and I am confident in my body and its ability

to get pregnant. I feel _____
(fill in the blank with three, four, or five feel good emotions like:
eager, excited, happy, and grateful) and feeling those feelings
feels good. I have the power to change MY health and improve
MY fertility and I am doing it NOW.

Read the above statement out loud, each and every day. Write it everywhere, e-mail it to yourself, record yourself saying it, and listen to it daily and start telling your friends about it. *Change your story.*

Even if you don't believe your new story or the statement above, write it and say it until you do. Each time you start to tell your old story, stop yourself and think of your new story. This isn't an overnight, fix it and be done type of thing; this is a process. This is a daily mantra. Choosing to believe in the power you have in all of this and in your beliefs is just as important as eating chicken eggs every day. Without joy and confidence, conception will be more difficult than it needs to be. As well, you deserve to tell a better story. You deserve to have joy, to be confident, to feel at peace in your life, *and* your future children deserve a parent who has those qualities. That is why you are going to start focusing on joy, *each and every day.*

Meditation and Visualization

There is good science to back up how meditation and visualization techniques can reduce stress, improve emotional states, and increase pregnancy rates in women who are trying to conceive. A very impressive study out of the Mind–Body Medicine Institute at Harvard University took 185 women who had been trying to conceive for one to two years and split them into groups: either a 10-week mind–body group, a 10-week support group, or a routine care control group. The birth rates during the one-year follow up period were as follows: Mind–body group, 55%; support group, 54%; and control group, 20%. Basically, women who meditated and participated in a support group were almost three times more likely to become pregnant than those that didn't do either. In addition the mind–body patients reported significantly greater psychological improvements than the support or control patients.

> Women who meditated and participated in a support group were almost three times more likely to become pregnant than those that didn't do either, according to a Mind–Body Medicine Institute study.

So improving your fertility is not only about your diet being organic or getting support from friends, family, this book, or a health professional: improving your fertility and stepping into your fertile goddess shoes is about you using the power of meditation and visualization to rejuvenate your fertility. One of my favorite tools is what I like to call mindful daydreaming.

Mindful Daydreaming

Get out that pen and paper again and put it aside for a few minutes. Find a quiet place where you can sit comfortably and really tune in to your body and your emotions. I'd like you to close your eyes and do a little daydreaming about seeing a positive pregnancy test. Sit and imagine it. Imagine peeing on that stick, waiting for it to dry, and seeing a positive result. Ask yourself: How would you feel emotionally? How would you feel physically? Would you start dancing right there in your bathroom? Would you cry? Would you scream? Would you run to grab your phone to call your partner? Set the timer on your phone and spend two solid, quiet, and committed minutes on this daydreaming moment. Try to stay in the moment of a positive pregnancy test. If you sense yourself deviating to a negative thought or a feeling of disbelief, gently bring yourself back to a positive pregnancy test. Two minutes daydreaming, seeing, and feeling yourself in the moment of a positive pregnancy test. Take your two minutes of positive pee-stick daydreaming now.

Good job. Now that you have spent your two minutes daydreaming about how good you would feel to get a positive pee-stick pregnancy test, I want you to write down five *positive* emotions you felt in the aftermath of your daydreaming. Here are some sample positive emotion words:

1. *Joy*
2. *Elation*

3. *Excitement*
4. *Happy*
5. *Bliss*

The key with this exercise is to do it so often that you believe what you were daydreaming is about to be a reality. See it. Feel it. Believe it.

Let's take a few more turns at this daydreaming exercise so you really get it. Choose one or more of the following scenarios and daydream your way into belief. I'd like you to imagine yourself:

- Very pregnant (belly bulging, feet swollen, back aching, pelvis hurting pregnant)
- Holding your newborn baby
- Being a mother

I'd love for you to do the two-minute mindful daydreaming exercise for each and every one of the above moments. Get into it, like *really* into it. Daydream away. No one is watching. Afterward, write down the emotions you experienced during the daydream session (and any ones you experienced after). If any negative emotions come up, just combat them with a positive one. This mindful daydreaming exercise is a really great fertility tool. It can help propel you into an *I am confident of my fertility* place and away from a fearful place. Daydream as often as you can about being fertile, pregnant, and becoming a mother. Find the feeling place of experiencing those things. Find the *oh, it feels so good* place of being where you want to be in your life: brimming with pregnancy. Find the belief that, in time, all that you want will be yours. The key to allowing these things to flow into your life is to be in a place of joyous, peaceful, confident belief *more* than you are in the place of negative, fertility-hindering disbelief. That's the key. My recommendation is that you mindfully daydream for two minutes each and every day. For me, I usually do the mindful daydreaming while I'm just waking up. I snooze my alarm and just let my mind mindfully daydream.

Meditating or Taking a Chill-Out Break

In addition, I am going to urge you to meditate for five to ten minutes *every single day*. Chilling out, or meditating, or sitting and breathing, whatever you want to call it, has the most outstandingly positive effects on health. Research out of the Benson–Henry Institute for Mind Body Medicine at Massachusetts General Hospital and Beth Israel

Deaconess Medical Center found that eliciting what the lead researcher calls the relaxation response (a physiologic state of deep rest induced by practices such as meditation, yoga, deep breathing, and prayer) can produce immediate changes in the expression of genes involved in immune function, energy metabolism, and insulin secretion as well as alleviating symptoms of anxiety and many other disorders. Another study published in *The Journal of Clinical Endocrinology & Metabolism* found that meditation regulated stress hormones in women.

What this means is that meditation not only helps to balance the stress hormones that can and will affect your fertility, but it will help you sleep more soundly and feel less stressed, anxious, and depressed. Taking time each day to meditate or just chill-out, not only helps women get pregnant faster, but also brings them health and relaxation. It's literally the best way to de-stress and anti-age, it's free, and you can do it anywhere. Here's how:

Find yourself a secluded and quiet place. At home this may be the living room couch or your bedroom. At work this could be your office, the bathroom, or on a walk in a nearby park.

- Silence your cell phone and turn off any other electronics so that they cannot interrupt you.
- Set the alarm on your phone (or computer or alarm clock) for 5 to 10 minutes (or for however long you want to chill-out for).
- Sitting comfortably, with your shoulders dropped and your jaw and fists relaxed, rest your hands on your lap, palms up toward the sky.
- Close your eyes or fixate them on something such as a picture on the wall.
- Breathe. This breathing is the deep, deeeeeep breathing kind. I want you to breathe so deeply that your belly rises. The breathing cycle should be: deep breath in (three to four seconds), belly rise, hold for a count of two seconds, then a long slow exhale (again, three to four seconds). For the first couple of times, try resting one of your hands on your abdomen so that you can feel it rise and fall with each breath. Nice and slowly.

Taking your daily chill-out time is deeply restorative and nourishing. And you deserve to cut out of your life for 5 to 10 minutes a day and mentally rejuvenate your health and fertility. For my chill-out time, I usually try to fit that in after my shower or sometimes during my lunch break.

To do both mindful daydreaming and meditating each day really only requires 7 to 12 minutes of your time. Do it. Your fertility will thank you.

> For those of you who prefer guided meditation, try using one of my favorites from Circle + Bloom (found on www.YesICanGetPregnant.com). They have downloadable meditations and visualizations geared specifically for fertility. Many of my patients love Circle + Bloom's products. I highly recommend them.

Yoga Mudras

The word *mudra* is a Sanskrit word that means "seal." Yoga mudras, like the ones below, are a nonverbal mode of communication used to seal or affirm an idea or intention. These hand and finger positions are to be incorporated during a meditation on an intention or desire; using the mudra seals the intention or desire. In the practice of yoga, mudras invoke divine power in the mind. Your flourishing fertile goddess deserves divine power in her mind. Practice these mudras along with your daydreaming exercise or with the specific yoga for fertility movements I describe below. There is a mudra and a movement for each specific phase of your menstrual cycle.

> My thanks to fertility yoga expert Karon Shovers Goldsmith for choosing the best mudra for each phase of the menstrual cycle and for the information on the yoga poses mentioned below. For more information, visit her website, http://karonshovers.com.

Menstruation Phase Mudra

The menstruation phase mudra is called the *Anjali Mudra*. Since the menstruation phase corresponds with the season of winter (as discussed in chapter 4), it is important during this time to be reflective, introspective, and nourishing to your body, your child's palace, and yourself. The gesture of the Anjali Mudra represents a devotion to the self, invoking an intention to be centered and calm at the place of your heart. As you hold this mudra gesture, it seals the energy in your body with the relationship to your divine self, your fertile goddess.

Instructions: Join palms evenly in front of your heart. The base of the thumbs can touch the center of the sternum, between the breasts. The other fingers point away from your heart (like you are holding your hands in prayer at the center of your chest). With your hands in this position, send love to yourself and to your child's palace (recall that the heart is intimately connected to your child's palace), by gently saying:

I love you. I send peace and love to my fertile child's palace.

Follicular Phase Mudra

The mudra for the follicular phase is called the *Prithivi Mudra* or the *Earth Mudra*. It is perfect for this phase of your cycle because as your body begins to grow follicles and a thicker uterine lining, this mudra will give you a feeling of grounding, stability, and security. It is said that this mudra invokes the energy of a seed in the ground that blossoms upward and outward with enthusiasm and joy.

Instructions: Touch or press together the tips of the thumb and ring finger, using gentle pressure. Do this with both hands. As you practice this mudra, send aspiring and enlivening energy to your ovaries and the growing follicles within them and say:

I send you love and fertile energy to grow and blossom.

Ovulation Phase Mudra

The ovulation phase mudra is called *Shakti Mudra* or the *Life Energy Mudra*. This mudra is meant to bring creative, expansive, and playful energy to you and relaxation into your pelvic region, which is perfect for the time of ovulation. At this phase, you want your pelvic region relaxed and open to receiving sperm and you want your emotional state to be creative and playful. Practicing the Shakti Mudra will make you feel expansive, playful, wild, free, and creative.

Instructions: Place both your right and left ring fingers and little fingers together (keep them extended but still soft) so they join one another. The other fingers are loosely bent over your thumbs, which are placed in your palms. As you practice this mudra, send joy and excitement to both your ovulated egg and your partner's sperm, envisioning them playing creatively together and say:

I am open to receiving love, joy, and fertility.

Luteal Phase Mudra

The luteal phase mudra is called *Pushan Mudra* or *Sustenance Mudra*. This mudra is absolutely perfect for the luteal phase, as it symbolizes accepting and receiving with the gesture of one hand, and letting things flow with the other. It has a relaxing effect and calms the nervous system. It also sustains and nourishes emotional balance.

Instructions: Position your right hand so the tips of the thumb, index finger, and middle finger touch together. The other fingers are extended. Position your left hand so the tips of the thumb, middle finger, and ring finger are touching. The index finger and small finger are extended. As you practice this mudra, send love and acceptance to your child's palace, saying:

Child's palace, you are lovingly fertile and accepting of my future child.

I hope that you find the time during each phase of your menstrual cycle to practice these mudras. Ideally, you should practice them two to three times during each phase. If it works for you, practice them with one of the two yoga-for-your-fertile-goddess poses described below.

Yoga

These two yoga poses bring an increase of energy, blood flow, and fertile Qi into the pelvis and open your chest—important both for breathing in healthy Qi, but also for opening your heart and releasing any anxiety or stress. All of your mudras can be practiced in these postures, according to whatever phase you are in during your monthly menstrual cycle.

Supta Baddha Konasana or Supported Bound Angle Pose

For this pose you will need a few props:

1 bolster (you can use a thick blanket, rolled up into a cigar shape)
2 pillows
1 single-fold blanket (a thin blanket folded over once)
1 eye pillow (optional)

Sit in front of the short end of the bolster (or a thick rolled-up blanket), about an inch from your tailbone.

Bring the souls of the feet together and place one pillow under each thigh for support.

Use your arms for support as you gently lie back onto the bolster, so that the center of the bolster runs along the center of your spine. If you feel any discomfort in your back, you can adjust the height of the bolster with an additional blanket or pillow. You can also place a single-fold blanket (or another pillow) under your head, making sure your forehead is higher than your chin and your chin is higher than your breastbone. Place your eye pillow over your eyes, if you wish.

Lie in this position for 5 to 10 minutes. Take this time to do some mindful daydreaming exercises or just lie there and meditate on sending love and openness to your child's palace.

Viparita Karani or Legs up the Wall Pose

The recommended props for this pose are:

1 four-fold blanket (a blanket folded over four times) or two pillows piled on top of one another
1 eye pillow (optional)

Place the left side of your body next to a wall and your feet on the floor.

Using your hands for support, shift your weight onto the outer right hip, then lower your right shoulder to the ground so that you can pivot your pelvis and sweep your legs up the wall.

Settle your back onto the floor, aligning your spine so that an imaginary line drawn from your nose to your navel would be perpendicular to the baseboard. There should be ample room for your shoulder blades to rest comfortably on the ground, and just enough space between your hips and the wall to allow your tailbone to dip gently toward the floor.

Once you are settled and centered, bend your knees and place your feet on the wall. Using your legs, lift your hips off the floor and place your blanket or pillows under your pelvis.

Cover yourself with a blanket for warmth, if you need one.

You can also place a small roll under the neck or a single-fold blanket.

Place your eye pillow. Relax.

Hold this pose for 5 to 10 minutes. Take this time to do some mindful daydreaming or just lie there and meditate on sending love and openness to your child's palace.

Variation: This pose can also be done on a chair:

Begin by sitting on the floor with a chair in front of you. You can place a folded blanket underneath you for comfort.

Lie back and place the lower legs on the chair seat so the knees are bent and the hips are bent.

Cover yourself with a blanket for warmth, if you need one.

You can also place a small roll under the neck or a single-fold blanket.

Place your eye pillow. Relax.

Hold this pose for 5 to 10 minutes. Take this time to do some mindful daydreaming or just lie there and meditate on sending love and openness to your child's palace.

If you have any concerns or questions on doing either of these poses properly without injury, speak to a yoga professional. If you have any previous injuries, consult your board-certified medical professional.

I gave you a lot of tips and tools in this chapter, and it is my hope that you will take the time your emotional self deserves to practice some or all of these tools every day. The key here is to believe more than you don't believe; have joy more than sorrow; peace more than anger; and confidence more than fear. Find joy in every day and confidently pursue your self-love health mission because it feels good. Take time to chill out—spend time mindfully daydreaming about your life and how you want it to be. Use your mudras, sit and send love to your child's palace while you gently hold your fertility-enhancing yoga poses. As much as it is important for you to identify the feelings that are holding you back, choose to let them go and replace them with their positive counterparts. By doing so, you will propel your health and your fertility forward.

8
Pulling It Together: A 7-Day Step-by-Step Fertility Rejuvenation Plan

You have come so far. I am hopeful that you have digested all of the information thus far and have already started making some fertility-rejuvenating lifestyle changes. This self-love health mission of yours will deliver results. You will feel healthier and your skin will glow and you will love all of it. This chapter is going to give you all the information you need to start living the *Yes, You Can Get Pregnant* lifestyle. I have mapped out for you seven days of what to eat, when to meditate, what mantras to practice, and everything you will need to know to fully embrace your self-love health mission.

The *Yes You Can Get Pregnant* Fertility Rejuvenation Plan requires that you do the following 10 things *every single day:*

1. Get seven to eight hours of uninterrupted sleep.
2. Eat within the first 30 minutes of waking and eat every two to three hours after that.
3. Meditate, mindful daydream, and do your mantras.
4. Exercise to maintain your healthy and fertile BMI.
5. "Lights out" an hour before bed (meaning all electronics are off).
6. Have hot sex (ideally four to five nights a week).
7. Keep your child's palace warm.
8. Avoid fertility-reducing environmental toxins and endocrine-disrupting chemicals.

9. Take your supplements every day.

10. Follow the *Yes, You Can Get Pregnant* diet:

- ○ Say NO to gluten, soy, added sugar, artificial sweeteners, genetically modified organism foods, and pesticides.
- ○ Say YES to animal protein, fat, vegetables, and fruits.

Yes, You Can Get Pregnant Diet Quick Tips

Per Day	Per Week
Healthy oils: 1–2 tbsp	Eggs: 8–10
Nuts and seeds: 2 tbsp	Meat: 4–6 servings*
Fruit: 1–2 servings (limit high-sugared fruits to 2–4/wk)	Fish: 6–10 servings*
Vegetables: 3–5 servings* (limit fresh veggie juice to 1–2/wk)	Liver: 3–4 oz (or take 2 liver pills/day)
Fermented foods: 1–2 tbsp	Chicken: 1–2 servings*
Bone broth: 8 oz 3–4 times	Full-fat dairy: 4 oz 2 times
Fish roe: 1 oz 1–2 times	Butter: 4 tbsp

*A serving size is about 3 oz or the size of your palm.

Go to www.YesICanGetPregnant.com to download the *Yes, You Can Get Pregnant* diet weekly checklist to stay on track with your diet and supplements.

Day One (*Note*: This schedule is based on a 7:00 a.m. wakeup and an 11:00 p.m. bedtime, but you should adjust to your own schedule for waking and sleeping).

7:00 a.m.   Wake up feeling refreshed and grateful for a great night's sleep.

7:00–7:03 a.m.   Say your child's palace mantra to yourself: *Dear Uterus, you are the palace of my child and I believe in you. I send you love and joy. You are a beautiful palace, brimming with*

Work these recommendations into your normal daily routine. At first this may require some adjustments to your schedule but your fertility and health will greatly benefit by following this lifestyle plan.

fertility and I fully believe in your ability to get pregnant. Then, spend two minutes in a mindful daydream about how exciting it is going to be to be a mother.

7:05 a.m.   Take your probiotics.

7:30 a.m.   *Breakfast:* Two scrambled eggs with tomato, spinach, and fresh basil, and a slice of gluten-free bread; after you've finished breakfast, take the rest of your supplements.

7:50 a.m.   Take a five-minute chill-out break. Practice sending joy and love to your child's palace with the Qi Gong exercise on page 153.

7:55 a.m.   Just before you leave your house, take a quick look in the mirror and look into your eyes and say: *I have the power to change MY health and improve MY fertility.*

10:00 a.m.   *Snack:* A half-cup of organic blueberries mixed with 1 tablespoon of gelatin and 3 ounces of full-fat Greek yogurt. (If you should be skipping dairy, then use coconut or almond milk yogurt. Be sure to check the sugar content and try to use one that doesn't have added sugars.)

11:30 a.m.   Get outside for a quick 5 to 10 minute walk to soak in some sunshine (even if it's cold out).

12:30 p.m.   *Lunch:* Mixed mesclun green salad with wild salmon (or sardines), onions, green beans, olives, a tablespoon of fermented veggies (or sauerkraut), olive oil, and vinegar.

12:45 p.m.   Take a moment and do a "one with nature" mental scan of your body. Tune into how you are feeling. Are you tensed? Tired? Feeling great? Whatever it is, tune into your body.

3:00 p.m.   *Snack:* One grapefruit and one handful (about 1 ounce) of almonds or cashews.

6:00 p.m.   *Dinner:* One baked chicken breast with fresh herbs, olive oil sautéed kale with garlic, and a sweet potato with 1 teaspoon of butter. Eat with a friend or your partner and share the best part of your day.

7:00 p.m.   It's time for another "one with nature" mental body scan. How are you feeling?

9:30 p.m.   One teaspoon of nut butter or three almonds or a quarter-cup of almond or coconut milk (just a little nibble to keep your blood sugar even while you sleep).

10:00 p.m.   "Lights out," meaning all electronics off and start getting ready for bed. Spend time in your bedroom journaling about five things that brought you joy today. Say your mantra to yourself: *I have the power to change MY health and improve MY fertility.* Think positive thoughts, spend intimate time with your partner talking, cuddling, or having hot sex.

11:00 p.m.   Time for sleep.

Day Two

7:00 a.m.   Wake up feeling rested. Be grateful and know that today is going to be a great day.

7:00–7:03 a.m.   Say your child's palace mantra to yourself: *Dear Uterus, you are the palace of my child and I believe in you. I send you love and joy. You are a beautiful palace, brimming with fertility and I fully believe in your ability to get pregnant.* Then, spend two minutes in a mindful daydream about how your day today is going to be filled with joy and fun. It'll be an easy, breezy, stressless day.

7:05 a.m.   Take your probiotics.

7:20 a.m.   *Breakfast:* One hardboiled egg and a half-cup of gluten-free hot cereal with half a banana (or a half-cup of blueberries), and a teaspoon of raw honey; after you've finished your breakfast, take the rest of your supplements.

7:35 a.m.   Take a five-minute chill-out break. Tune into your body and send love to yourself. Take a few moments while you're taking your morning shower to do one of your fertile goddess Qi Gong exercises.

7:55 a.m.   Just before you leave your house, take a quick look in the mirror and look into your eyes and say: *I have the power to change MY health and improve MY fertility.*

10:00 a.m.   *Snack:* A quarter-cup (or 2 ounces) of hummus with celery sticks.

11:00 a.m. Tune in to your body and take a two-minute chill-out break.

12:30 a.m. *Lunch:* two organic, grass-fed (pork or turkey) sausages sautéed in 1 tablespoon of coconut oil or butter, 1 cup of roasted veggies (such as Brussels sprouts and beets).

1:00 p.m. Sneak outside for five minutes to breathe in some fresh air. Tune in to your body and ask yourself: "How am I feeling today?"

3:30 p.m. *Snack:* Two cups of cut-up melon with 1 tablespoon of gelatin sprinkled on it. While you're snacking, think a positive thought such as: I love my self-love health mission.

5:30 p.m. Take a walk or get in some exercise.

6:30 p.m. *Dinner:* Three ounces of pan-seared (in 1 tablespoon of butter) beef tenderloin with olive oil–sautéed spinach, Brussels sprouts and garlic, and a half-cup brown rice. Flavor with juice from half a lemon and a dash of sea salt. Spend some quality time this evening doing something you love: read a book, watch your favorite show, take a bath, make love to your partner.

9:30 p.m. One teaspoon of nut butter or three almonds or a quarter-cup of almond or coconut milk (just a little nibble to keep your blood sugar even while you sleep).

10:00 p.m. All electronics off. Take a few minutes to write down the five things that brought you joy today. Chill out and get to bed early.

11:00 p.m. Bedtime.

Day Three

7:00 a.m. Wake up feeling rested. Be grateful and know that today is going to be a great day.

7:00–7:03 a.m. Say your child's palace mantra to yourself: *Dear Uterus, you are the palace of my child and I believe in you. I send you love and joy. You are a beautiful palace, brimming with fertility, and I fully believe in your ability to get pregnant.* Then spend two minutes in a mindful daydream about being pregnant and how insanely happy you will be.

7:05 a.m. Take your probiotics.

7:20 a.m. *Breakfast:* A smoothie with a half-cup of coconut milk, 1 cup of water, 1 tablespoon of gelatin, 1 tablespoon of raw cacao powder, and 1 tablespoon of organic nut butter (yum!); after you've finished your breakfast, take the rest of your supplements.

7:35 a.m.   Take a five-minute chill-out break. Tune into you body and do one of the menstrual mudras (depending on where you are in your menstrual cycle; refer to chapter 7).

7:55 a.m.   Just before you leave your house, take a quick look in the mirror and look into your eyes and say: *I have the power to change MY health and improve MY fertility.*

10:00 a.m.   *Snack:* Half of a Lärabar (see my list of great, pack-aged, on-the-go snacks on page 190).

11:00 a.m.   Take a moment and do a "one with nature" mental scan of your body. Tune into how you are feeling? Are you tensed? Tired? Feeling great? Whatever it is, tune into your body.

1:00 p.m.   *Lunch:* Watercress greens (or spinach or raw kale) with 3 ounces of grilled salmon (or canned light tuna), half an avocado, raw or cooked mushrooms (shitake, maitake, or black), 1 tablespoon of raw organic sunflower seeds, 1 table-spoon of olive oil and vinegar. Flavor with some fresh ground pepper.

2:00 p.m.   Get a dose of sunshine (and a break from work) by tak-ing a quick walk outside. Notice the environment around you: the trees, the sky, the smiles on people's face. Smile back at everyone you see.

3:30 p.m.   *Snack:* the other half of your Lärabar.

4:00 p.m.   Take a moment to tune into your body. How are you feeling? Repeat your mantra in your head: *I have the power to change MY health and improve MY fertility.*

6:30 p.m.   *Dinner:* Pan-sautéed filet of sole with shallots and leeks, a quarter-cup of cooked quinoa with rosemary, and 1 table-spoon of olive oil and steamed asparagus. Garnish with 1 table-spoon of fish roe and the juice from half of a lemon.

7:30 p.m.   Spend 10 to 15 minutes in one of the fertility-enhancing yoga poses. Take this time to send loving thoughts to your heart and to your child's palace. Visualize your child's palace being receptive, open, and joyful.

9:00 p.m.   Make chicken soup for your lunch tomorrow. With love. (See recipe on pages 193–194.)

9:30 p.m.   One teaspoon of nut butter or 3 almonds or a quarter-cup of almond or coconut milk (just a little nibble to keep your blood sugar even while you sleep).

10:00 p.m.   All electronics off. Take a few minutes to write down the five things that brought you joy today. Do a mental "one with nature" body scan and check in with how you are feeling. Have hot sex with your partner.

11:00 p.m.   Bedtime. Sleep tight.

Day Four

7:00 a.m.   Wake up feeling rested and happy.

7:00–7:03 a.m.   Say your child's palace mantra to yourself: *Dear Uterus, you are the palace of my child and I believe in you. I send you love and joy. You are a beautiful palace, brimming with fertility and I fully believe in your ability to get pregnant.* Then spend two minutes in a mindful daydream about something in your life that you want that is not fertility related (maybe that new job or how it feels to be sitting on a beach on that island you want to visit).

7:05 a.m.   Take your probiotics.

7:20 a.m.   *Breakfast:* Two eggs over-easy with half an avocado; after you've finished your breakfast, take the rest of your supplements.

7:35 a.m.   Take a five-minute chill-out break making sure your neck, jaw, and shoulders are relaxed.

7:55 a.m.   Just before you leave your house, take a quick look in the mirror and look into your eyes and say: *I have the power to change MY health and improve MY fertility.*

10:00 a.m.   *Snack:* Two ounces of homemade liver pate (see recipe on page 199) on a slice of gluten-free toast.

11:00 a.m.   Get some fresh air, even if only for a few minutes.

12:30 p.m.   *Lunch:* A bowl of homemade chicken soup with a half-cup of cooked quinoa.

1:00 p.m.   Send a message to someone you love and tell him or her how wonderful they are.

3:30 p.m.   *Snack:* A sliced apple, 2 tablespoons of almond butter.

4:30 p.m.   Take a mental "one with nature" body scan. How are you feeling? Repeat your mantra in your head: *I have the power to change MY health and improve MY fertility.*

5:30 p.m.   Smile and think of one thing you're grateful for.

6:30 p.m.   *Dinner:* One cup of quinoa pasta with two turkey meatballs (about 2 ounces of ground turkey) in organic tomato sauce (1/2-cup) with a sprinkle of gelatin and 1 tablespoon of organic parmesan cheese. Share laughs with a friend.

8:30 p.m.   Cook your lunch for tomorrow.

9:30 p.m.   One teaspoon of nut butter or three almonds or a quarter-cup of almond or coconut milk (just a little nibble to keep your blood sugar even while you sleep).

10:00 p.m.   All electronics off. Take a few minutes to write down the five things that brought you joy today. Do a mental "one with nature" body scan and check in with how you are feeling. Spend time relaxing and doing nothing. It's a great time to unwind.

11:00 p.m.   Bedtime. Sleep tight.

Day Five

7:00 a.m.   Wake up feeling rested and grateful knowing that today is going to be a great day.

7:00–7:03 a.m.   Say your child's palace mantra to yourself: *Dear Uterus, you are the palace of my child and I believe in you. I send you love and joy. You are a beautiful palace, brimming with fertility and I fully believe in your ability to get pregnant.* Then spend two minutes in a mindful daydream about that positive pee-stick pregnancy test you are going to experience really soon!

7:05 a.m.   Take your probiotics.

7:20 a.m.   *Breakfast:* One fried egg with one piece of bacon and a grapefruit; after you've finished your breakfast, take the rest of your supplements.

7:35 a.m.   Take a five-minute chill-out break doing the mudra for this phase of your menstrual cycle.

7:55 a.m.   Just before you leave your house, take a quick look in the mirror and look into your eyes and say: *I have the power to change MY health and improve MY fertility.*

10:00 a.m.   *Snack:* A quarter-cup (2 ounces) of hummus (see recipe on page 198) and celery.

12:30 p.m.   *Lunch:* Mixed green salad with salmon, kidney beans, corn, half of an avocado, tomato, olives, fermented veggies, with 1 tablespoon of olive oil and vinegar.

1:30 p.m.   Sneak outside for a dose of sunshine. While you're out there take a moment and text yourself five reasons why you love yourself.

3:30 p.m.   *Snack:* Eight ounces of vegetable juice (beets, spinach, ginger, celery, and carrot).

4:00 p.m.   Be grateful and take a mental "one with nature" moment to check in and see how you're feeling.

6:30 p.m.   *Dinner:* Baked pork chop with fresh parsley and thyme, corn on the cob, and sautéed green beans with sliced almonds.

8:30 p.m.   Make the summer squash pancakes that you'll have for breakfast tomorrow and the next day.

9:30 p.m.   One teaspoon of nut butter or three almonds or a quarter-cup of almond or coconut milk or half of a hardboiled egg (just a little nibble to keep your blood sugar even while you sleep).

10:00 p.m.   All electronics off. Spend 10 to 15 minutes in one of the yoga for fertility poses. Send love and joy to your child's palace.

11:00 p.m.   Bedtime. Spend some intimate time with your partner and have some hot sex.

Don't Go Overboard with Packaged Gluten-Free Foods

A lot of the gluten-free packaged products available, such as crackers, cereals, and snack foods, are processed and contain ingredients that can affect your fertility (such as sugar and soy!)

So, try and limit yourself to five servings per week of packaged gluten-free foods and be sure to read the ingredients.

Check out page 190 for my favorite "Aimee Approved" packaged gluten-free products.

Day Six

7:00 a.m.   Wake up feeling rested and grateful knowing that today is going to be a great day.

7:00–7:03 a.m.   Say your child's palace mantra to yourself: *Dear Uterus, you are the palace of my child and I believe in you. I send you love and joy. You are a beautiful palace, brimming with fertility and I fully believe in your ability to get pregnant.* Then spend two minutes in a mindful daydream about how wonderful of a parent your partner is going to be. See it, feel it, believe it.

7:05 a.m.   Take your probiotics.

7:20 a.m.   *Breakfast:* Two summer squash pancakes (see recipe on pages 200–201; they are delicious!) topped with half an avocado; after you've finished your breakfast, take the rest of your supplements.

7:35 a.m.   Take a five-minute chill-out break. If you downloaded the Circle+Bloom fertility-guided meditations, listen to one of them (YesICanGetPregnant.com).

7:55 a.m.   Just before you leave your house, take a quick look in the mirror and look into your eyes and say: *I have the power to change MY health and improve MY fertility.*

10:00 a.m.   *Snack:* One Go Raw bar.

11:00 a.m.   Send a fun, sexy message to your partner.

12:30 p.m.   *Lunch:* Kale salad with a quarter-cup of hummus, sesame seeds, olives, olive oil, and balsamic vinegar.

2:00 p.m.   Get outside. Take a moment to focus on something you are grateful for.

3:00 p.m.   *Snack:* A cup of berries or an apple with a handful (1 ounce) of almonds.

4:30 p.m.   Look into a mirror and say your mantra: *I have the power to change MY health and improve MY fertility.*

6:30 p.m.   *Dinner:* A half-cup of quinoa pasta with broccoli rabe and shitake mushrooms, topped with 1 tablespoon of butter and 1 teaspoon of grated cheese. Do something fun tonight; go out with your partner or a good friend. Or just take some time to dance in your house to your favorite song. Have fun. Enjoy this beautiful life you are living.

9:30 p.m.   One teaspoon of nut butter or three almonds or a quarter-cup of almond or coconut milk (just a little nibble to keep your blood sugar even while you sleep).

10:00 p.m.   All electronics off. Journal about five things that brought you joy today. Read an inspiring, positive, uplifting book. Chill out and check in with your body. How is it feeling?

11:00 p.m.   Bedtime. Night, night.

Day Seven

7:00 a.m.   Wake up feeling rested and grateful knowing that today is going to be a great day.

7:00–7:03 a.m.   Say your child's palace mantra to yourself: *Dear Uterus, you are the palace of my child and I believe in you. I send you love and joy. You are a beautiful palace, brimming with fertility and I fully believe in your ability to get pregnant.* Then spend two minutes in a mindful daydream about how fun it'll be to play with your future child on the beach. Believe it. Feel it. See it happening.

7:05 a.m.   Take your probiotics.

7:20 a.m.   *Breakfast:* Two summer squash pancakes (leftover from yesterday's homemade batch); after you've finished breakfast, take the rest of your supplements.

7:35 a.m.   Take a five-minute chill-out break. Breathe deeply, picturing a bright, white, loving light running from your heart into your child's palace.

7:55 a.m.   Just before you leave your house, take a quick look in the mirror and look into your eyes and say: *I have the power to change MY health and improve MY fertility.*

10:00 a.m.   *Snack:* One cup of homemade chicken soup.

11:00 a.m.   Send a grati-text (an *I am grateful for you because* text message) to a good friend.

12:30 p.m.   *Lunch:* Coconut milk smoothie: a half-cup of coconut milk, 1 cup of water, 1 tablespoon of nut butter, 1 tablespoon of ground flaxseeds, and 1 cup of blueberries.

1:00 p.m.   Get outside for a healthy dose of fertility-rejuvenating vitamin D.

3:00 p.m.   *Snack:* An apple with 1 tablespoon of nut butter.

4:30 p.m.   Tell yourself five reasons why you think you are a wonderful human being.

6:30 p.m.   *Dinner:* One cup of homemade shrimp salad (see the recipe on pages 199–200) with 10 rice crackers (Edward and Son's is my favorite brand; see page 190 for some more of my favorite Aimee Approved brands).

7:30 p.m.   Start a batch of homemade bone broth.

9:30 p.m.   One teaspoon of nut butter or three almonds or a quarter-cup of almond or coconut milk or half a hardboiled egg (just a little nibble to keep your blood sugar even while you sleep).

10:00: p.m.   All electronics off. Journal about five things that brought you joy today. Spend some time laughing with your partner. Have some hot sex and love every moment of it.

11:00 p.m.   Bedtime.

Now you have all of the essential tools you need to rejuvenate your fertility and cultivate your inner fertile goddess. Turn the page for some more fertility-enhancing tips.

Part III
More Fertility-Enhancing Tips and Ways to Overcome Common Fertility Challenges

9
Additional Treatments to Enhance Fertility

You have learned so much thus far, and I know you are eager and ready to officially begin on your *Yes, You Can Get Pregnant* fertility rejuvenation program. In this chapter, I want to discuss some Traditional Oriental Medicine (TOM) odds and ends that I didn't get to fully address earlier. These are topics such as acupuncture and its success in treating fertility, Chinese herbs and why they are so useful in the treatment of female hormonal disorders, Qi Gong (a TOM mind–body practice) and its effectiveness in treating fertility challenges as well as mental–emotional distress, and lastly, why doing things such as keeping your child's palace warm and having hot sex is so important for your health and your fertility.

Acupuncture and Chinese Herbs

We have discussed TOM extensively throughout this book; however, I haven't mentioned much about acupuncture or Chinese herbs. That is not because I don't practice acupuncture and see clinical results from it, prescribe Chinese herbs, or believe they are extremely powerful substances that can definitely help improve your fertility. I do. However, I do not think it is ethical to generally recommend acupuncture points to use or Chinese herbs to take as each individual case is so entirely different. These modalities are very potent and should only be prescribed to you by a practitioner you are physically seeing in his or her office (or doing live consults with) who has extensively studied acupuncture and Chinese herbology and is certified by the National Certification Commission for Acupuncture and Oriental Medicine (NCCAOM). It is important to keep in mind that herbs, of any kind, should not be taken based on a recommendation by an employee of your local health food store or because a magazine suggested them. Additionally, recommending the use of acupuncture points or acupressure should also be left up to a professional whom you have direct contact with. Sure, there are acupressure points that can help with regulating your hormone levels, but encouraging you to use them on your own is not the best way to practice the medicine I studied and practiced for so many years.

With that said, using both acupuncture and Chinese herbs in regulating a woman's menstrual cycle and improving her fertility quotient is extremely beneficial. Both acupuncture and Chinese herbs have been used for centuries to improve blood flow and circulation to your child's palace. By inserting tiny needles in specific areas of your body, acupuncture has been scientifically proven to improve uterine blood flow and ovulation, regulate menstrual cycles, and curb PMS. Several articles have been published in the scientific journal *Fertility and Sterility* on the effects of acupuncture on a woman's menstrual cycle. Specifically, researchers have found that acupuncture can help with:

- Regulating the menstrual cycle
- Regulating and inducing ovulation
- Balancing the endocrine (hormonal) system
- Improving the blood flow to the pelvic cavity, specifically the uterus
- Increasing the chance of pregnancy for women undergoing in vitro fertilization (IVF)

And for your man, it has been shown to:

- Invigorate sperm
- Enhance sperm count and motility

Specific Chinese herbal formulations are also used in repairing and preparing your child's palace. Depending on your specific presentation, an NCCAOM board certified Chinese herbalist can make you your own special fertility-quotient-enhancing blend. Chinese herbs are prescrlbed according to specific herbal properties such as acupuncture meridian entered, functions, clinical use, major combinations, and dosage. Don't worry if it sounds complicated, board certified Chinese herbalists are up on the current pharmacological research on Chinese herbs including their potential drug interactions; antimicrobial, antiviral, and antifungal effect; and effects on blood pressure, smooth muscle, hormones, the central nervous system, and gynecology.

Remember: only go to a qualified and NCCAOM board certified acupuncturist and herbalist for treatment. Unfortunately, there are practitioners out there who are not as qualified to treat you as they should be. Be smart and check out the credentials of any and all medical professionals you seek the advice of. And DO NOT self-treat with Chinese herbs; being natural does not mean they are always safe.

Go to www.NCCAOM.org to find a qualified practitioner in your area or schedule a Skype consult with me at www.YesICanGetPregnant.com.

Qi Gong

Qi Gong is a type of meditative movement, a combination of slow movements with deep breathing and focused concentration, that has been a part of TOM for thousands of years. It is often recommended by TOM practitioners as an exercise that improves health and vitality. Qi Gong is a potent treatment for fertility and emotional distress. Through using breath with coordinated movements, this technique cultivates Qi in your body and supports the functioning of your reproductive system. It not only improves circulation and blood flow to your reproductive area but also improves sex drive and, as one of my professors put it, helps you achieve "orgasmic bliss." Sign me up!

Women in their 20s, 30s, and 40s need to focus on improving the health of their child's palace so conception can occur with ease. When you practice Qi Gong you tap into, balance, and enliven the flow of energy in your body. As Qi Gong is a meditative practice, it is also beneficial as it quiets the mind and allows stress to be eased while improving the flow of Qi, blood, and essence to your entire reproductive system. By practicing Qi Gong, you can breathe new life into and through your child's palace. I recommend you try some of these exercises and bring healthy, vital energy into your reproductive system.

Fertile Goddess Qi Gong Exercises

The following three Qi Gong exercises are said to improve Qi flow to your heart, child's palace, and kidneys to nourish your three vital substances for fertility: Qi, blood, and essence. It is said that it is best to practice Qi Gong between 7:00 and 9:00 a.m. or 7:00 and 9:00 p.m. outside in nature, but for now you should just practice it where you can, when you can. The more you practice these exercises the more you will be in touch with not only the natural rhythm of your body, but also with your Qi and how it flows through your fertile body. Often patients tell me the more they practice Qi Gong the more they can feel a sort of "buzz" or electrical current running through their body.

Open Your Heart

Instructions: Stand with feet shoulder-width apart and swing your arms at your sides up to the height of your mouth. Swing them in unison. Do this for at least three minutes. While you are swinging your arms, concentrate on energy flowing through your chest and your heart, opening your heart up to letting go of any anxiety and tension.

Invigorate Your Kidneys

Instructions: Take the palms of both your hands, place them over your kidneys (located below your rib cage on your back, on either side of your spine) and begin to rub them back and forth over your kidneys. As you rub, focus on the connection between your palms and your kidneys. The palms have to do with your heart, and by placing your palms over your kidneys and rubbing them you are creating a circuit between the heart and kidneys. This is bringing healthy blood flow to your child's palace as both the heart and the kidneys connect to your child's palace via their own individual channels. Do this for at least three minutes, focusing on sending fertile energy from your palms to your kidneys and your child's palace.

Another tip: Do this rubbing regularly and even on your partner before intercourse as this can help men maintain their erections, generate healthy sperm, and stave off premature ejaculation.

Send Joy and Love to Your Child's Palace

Instructions: In a comfortable, seated position, close your eyes and try to clear your mind. Place the tip of your tongue on the roof of your mouth just behind the top of your front teeth and breathe deeply in through your nose and concentrate on bringing your breath from your nose and down the midline of your body, between your breasts, down your abdomen, and to a region about two inches below your belly button.

As you continue breathing in, move your focus to the muscles of your genital area and below your navel to your uterus. While doing this, gently contract your pelvic floor muscles as if you were trying to stop urinating (this is called a Kegel). Relax your muscles and exhale fully from your abdomen while letting your focus return up the posterior midline of your body to the top of your head and back to your nose. Repeat this breathing exercise 10 times. As you are breathing in through your nose and down to your lower abdomen send love and joy to your child's palace. You can literally think of the words *love* and *joy* and nothing more, or you can think loving, joyous thoughts. Either will work.

Getting to Know the Kegel

Kegel exercises are great for getting healthy blood flow to your pelvic area and for strengthening the muscles around your vagina, uterus, and bladder. They're also good for having a better orgasm!

    Here's how you do them:

- First, you've got to strengthen the correct muscle. To figure out the right muscle pretend you are urinating and then deliberately stop the flow of urine.
- Then, isolate the muscle. While doing the Kegel, be sure to keep your back, abdominal, and thigh muscles

---

(continued)

(continued)

> relaxed so that you can isolate and concentrate more energy into the pelvic-floor muscles you are trying to strengthen.
>
> • "Kegel" away while lying or sitting with your knees together, squeeze your Kegel muscle and hold the squeeze for 10 seconds. Then relax the muscle for a few seconds. Do this 10 to 20 times in a row. Work up to three sessions a day. Don't hold your breath during exercise. Breathe slowly and deeply throughout each repetition.

The Importance of Hot Sex

In chapter 4, I talked about how important hot sex and orgasms are for you, especially when you are trying to conceive. We are going to talk about them a little bit more, because they are *that* important. Research shows that the contracting muscles in your pelvic area as a result of an orgasm help propel sperm up through the cervix and increase your odds of becoming pregnant. In TOM we also say the orgasm is important because it is a joyful experience, and you know by now—joy is key to fertility rejuvenation. As a reminder, one thing you must try not to lose sight of is: sex is fun and should be enjoyed. Sex is a beautiful experience shared by two individuals, and it should be intimate and sexy. Unfortunately, it can begin to lose its luster if all you're focused on is whether or not *this time* you're going to get pregnant. My recommendation: try and keep it hot and heavy. Do whatever works for you and your partner to get you both physically, chemically, and emotionally engaged in the act of sex. Don't use sex merely as a baby-making mechanism but as a way to connect to your partner.

Now that you have the fertility rejuvenation protocol all mapped out for you along with some extra fertility-enhancing tips, let's get into some specifics about the most commonly diagnosed Western medical fertility challenges women face, how they are linked to certain autoimmune diseases, and how to use the knowledge and power you now have to best overcome them.

10
Overcoming Common Fertility Challenges

At this point, you have the tools to rejuvenate your fertility, regulate your hormones, and balance your immune system *regardless* of what specific fertility issue or medical illness may be contributing to your situation; however, it is necessary that we discuss the most common fertility challenges that women are currently facing. Chances are if you have been trying to conceive for some time you have consulted with your doctor, discussed with your friends, and read *ad nauseum* online about all the possible things that could be *wrong* with your body. So before we get into this, I want to remind you: you are not broken. Sure, it is possible that there are a few kinks in your system but you can work them out. On the contrary, if you have already begun to follow the fertility rejuvenation program in this book, you are already helping your body work out some of these kinks. But I do believe there is tremendous power in using both an Eastern and Western approach to health, and that is why in this chapter I will guide you through the most common fertility challenges that women are facing.

Knowledge is power and the information in this chapter is meant to empower you so that you can make the best choices for your health and your fertility. More importantly, the information that follows will assist you in deciphering if you have any autoimmunity going on that could be causing or exacerbating your fertility challenges and affecting your ability to get pregnant. Remember: the current science is linking autoimmunity to the most common fertility issues, and the fertility-rejuvenation protocol laid out in this book is aimed at calming autoimmunity in addition to improving egg quality and overall reproductive health. However, going over the symptoms and diagnostics of most common fertility issues as well as the most predominant autoimmune diseases and how autoimmunity and fertility are being linked scientifically and causing reproductive disorders will give you even more power over your health. Let's dig in.

According to the American Society for Reproductive Medicine (ASRM) the four most common causes of female factor fertility issues, from a Western medical perspective, are:

1. *Ovulation dysfunction*: This occurs when a woman's reproductive system does not produce the proper amounts of hormones necessary to develop, mature, and release a healthy egg. The most common conditions that cause ovulation dysfunction are polycystic ovarian syndrome (PCOS) and premature ovarian aging (POA)
2. *Anatomical problems*: Abnormal development or function of the female anatomy can prevent the egg and the sperm from meeting. The most common anatomical problems are fallopian tube blockage (approximately 20% of all women with fertility issues have blocked fallopian tubes, usually as a result of endometriosis), uterine fibroids or polyps (noncancerous/benign masses that develop in the uterus), and pelvic scar tissue from previous surgeries (such as appendicitis, previous cesarean section, laparoscopy, and cervical biopsies) or infections.
3. *Endometriosis*: A condition wherein the tissue that lines the uterus develops outside the uterus, usually on other reproductive organs inside the pelvis or in the abdominal cavity.
4. *Immunological problems*: Autoimmune diseases such as autoimmune thyroid disease (AITD) and celiac disease (CD) have been on the rise over the past 20 years and are linked to many reproductive disorders. These autoimmune diseases cause a problem with a woman's immune system, which can lead to sperm rejection

or pregnancy loss. Antibodies (immune or protective proteins) in a woman's system can fail to recognize, and hence reject, sperm or an embryo, inhibiting conception and pregnancy.

Let's break down the most common fertility challenges:

PCOS

According to the ASRM, PCOS is the most common fertility challenge in the United States, affecting approximately 20% to 30% of all women with fertility issues. PCOS is a hormonal (too much testosterone and estrogen) and metabolic (abnormal blood sugar levels and/or insulin resistance) imbalance in the body that leads to ovulatory dysfunction. There is some controversy as to whether or not PCOS is actually an autoimmune disease; however, recent research published in 2007 in the journal *Autoimmune Review* stated, "A high concentration of antiovarian antibodies suggests that immune reaction is associated with PCOS; a high concentration of antisperm antibodies suggests an association of the two conditions with PCOS." This means there is some evidence that PCOS is an autoimmune disease and that it causes autoimmunity against ovaries and sperm. There also is a significantly higher incidence of PCOS in patients that also have either AITD or type 1 diabetes.

- Symptoms: Some women with PCOS present with no symptoms other than anovulation (lack of ovulation) or infrequent ovulations and infrequent menstrual periods. However, some common symptoms are: acne; weight gain; difficulty losing weight; excessive hair growth on face, neck, and breasts; patches of hair loss on the scalp; thinning scalp hair; hypoglycemia; visible cysts seen on the ovaries upon sonogram.
- Tests you need to ask your doctor to do:
  - Transvaginal ultrasound: if you are not ovulating regularly, or are experiencing infrequent menstrual cycles (coming every 45–100 days) you should request your doctor do a transvaginal ultrasound, which is a sonogram of your ovaries to check for cysts.
  - Hormone panel:
    - Free testosterone: should be between 0.3 and 1.9 ng/dL. In PCOS, free testosterone is usually elevated.

- Sex hormone binding globulin (SHBG): should be between 18 and 114 nmol/L. In PCOS, SHGB may be low.
- Dehydroepiandrosterone (DHEA-S): should be between 35 and 430 ug/dL. Most women with PCOS tend to have DHEA-S levels greater than 200 ug/dL.
- Follicle-stimulating hormone/luteinizing hormone (FSH/LH) ratio: should be a 1:1 ratio, but with PCOS a ratio of greater than 2:1 or 3:1 may be considered diagnostic.
- Thyroid panel: See above and be sure to check for thyroid antibodies as these two diseases are often found together.
- Prolactin: Should be less than 25 ng/mL. But this should be checked as high prolactin levels can indicate a problem with your pituitary gland.
- Glucose tolerance test (GTT): See above. In PCOS, it is usually high.
- Cholesterol: See above. In PCOS cholesterol is usually elevated.

- How to naturally manage symptoms: Follow the fertility rejuvenation protocol laid out in this book. In addition: avoid dairy, be sure to keep your blood sugar even by eating protein every two to three hours, make it a priority to meditate every day, and cut out coffee.

- What does it mean for your fertility: In order to get pregnant, you need to be ovulating. PCOS can be regulated naturally via the dietary recommendations in this book, reducing your exposure to environmental toxins, keeping your blood sugar even, and maintaining a healthy BMI. Once your hormones become balanced and you start ovulating on a regular basis, your odds of conceiving naturally are greatly increased.

Birth Control and Ovulation Disorders

If you have used birth control, your ovulation has been disrupted to prevent pregnancy. Birth control will affect your fertility once you stop taking it, and ovulation disorders are one of the leading causes of fertility issues. According

(continued)

(continued)

to a 2010 paper published in the journal *Contemporary Ob/ Gyn*, which reviewed many previous studies on various birth control methods and how they affected fertility after they were discontinued, the average time for a women to resume normal ovulation after discontinuing a contraceptive was:

- 3 to 6 months with oral contraceptive pills (OCPs)
- 3 to 4 months with intrauterine devices (IUDs)
- 10 months with depot medroxyprogesterone acetate (DMPA or Depo).

Based on this research, please take into account how this might affect how soon you conceive after stopping your method of contraception. But keep in mind, the protocol laid out in this book will help your body get back on track quickly after going off of your contraception. Follow the fertility-rejuvenation protocol and your body will start ovulating regularly.

POA

Premature ovarian aging (POA), also known as poor ovarian reserve, is when a woman has FSH levels above where they should be *at her age*, or her anti-Müllerlan hormone (AMH) levels are below where they should be for her age.

- Symptoms: Women with POA often have no symptoms at all (from a Western medical standpoint, although they usually have symptoms from an Eastern standpoint; more on that later in this chapter) other than difficulty conceiving.
- Blood tests you need to ask your doctor to do:
  - FSH: Levels should be tested on cycle day 2 or 3 of your menses:
    - Levels under 6 mIU/mL are considered excellent, from 6 to 9 mIU/mL is considered good, from 9 to 10 mIU/mL is considered fair, and above 11 mIU/mL is considered diminished ovarian reserve.
    - Keep in mind that FSH can change from one menstrual cycle to the next and is no longer considered the gold standard for ovarian reserve.

- AMH: These levels have been shown to be a much better determinant of fertility in comparison to FSH. AMH is produced directly by the ovarian follicles, and levels of AMH correlate with the number of antral follicles in the ovaries.
  - Levels should be between 0.7 ng/mL and 3.0 ng/mL; if AMH is above 3.0 ng/mL if can indicate PCOS. An AMH below 0.7 ng/mL can indicate poor ovarian reserve.
- Antral follicle count: this test is conducted via an ultrasound where your doctor actually counts the number of antral follicles seen in the ovary:
  - From 11 to 30 antral follicles is considered normal and a good sign of ample ovarian reserve; less than 11 antral follicles is considered a sign of POA; higher than 30 antral follicles can be indicative of PCOS.
- How to naturally manage symptoms: Follow the fertility rejuvenation protocol in this book, being sure to have your daily dose of bone broth as well as to eat caviar weekly, take a shot of wheat grass three to four times per week, and add royal jelly to your supplement regimen.
- What does this mean for your fertility: all it takes is one good egg to get pregnant. So even if your ovarian reserve is showing signs of diminishing, follow the recommendations in this book and believe in the power you have to change your health and your fertility. Your focus is to improve your egg quality, and this book is loaded with information on how to do just that. Remember: women with POA get pregnant all the time.

> The difference between POA and premature ovarian failure (POF), a loss of normal function of your ovaries before the age of 40, basically comes down to FSH levels. If FSH is high for your age but below 40 mIU/mL, then it is considered POA. If FSH is above 40 mIU/mL, then it is considered POF.

Endometriosis

Next to PCOS, the ASRM states that endometriosis is the second most common cause of fertility issues in women, affecting approximately 20% to 30% of women who are having a difficult time conceiving.

Endometriosis is a female health disorder that occurs when cells from the lining of the uterus, the endometrial lining, grow in other areas of the body such as the ovaries, intestines, and fallopian tubes. With each monthly menstruation, this endometrial tissue responds to the fluctuation in hormones and can cause menstrual pain, internal bleeding, heavy menstrual bleeding, scar tissue buildup, blocked fallopian tubes, and difficulty conceiving. Because endometriosis is the most common cause of anatomical problems that can lead to fertility challenges, if you are dealing with any anatomical or structural fertility challenges follow these endometriosis recommendations.

As with PCOS, there is some controversy over whether or not endometriosis is an autoimmune condition; however, research published in 2012 from the journal *Autoimmunity Reviews* stated: "In some of these women [with endometriosis] there are also a chronic local inflammatory process and presence of autoantibodies. It is not known whether this process is part of the etiology or is a secondary response to the ectopic cells. Furthermore, endometriosis shares similarities with several autoimmune diseases." Another paper published in the journal *Fertility and Sterility* concluded that "substantial evidence indicates that endometriosis at least shares many similarities with autoimmune diseases."

- Symptoms: Some women have very severe symptoms and some women have no symptoms at all. Common symptoms include: very painful menstrual cramps (pain may get worse over time), chronic pain in the lower back and pelvis, pain during or after sex, intestinal pain, painful bowel movements or painful urination during menstrual periods, spotting or bleeding between menstrual periods, difficulty getting pregnant, fatigue, diarrhea, constipation, bloating, or nausea, especially during menstrual periods.
- Tests you need to ask your doctor to do: it is difficult to definitively diagnose endometriosis.
  - Laparoscopy: If your doctor suspects endometriosis, laparoscopic surgery will likely be recommended to confirm the presence of endometriosis. *Note: I'm not advocating laparoscopy as it can be unnecessary in many cases and the endometriosis grows back soon after it's been removed.*
  - Pelvic MRI: A less invasive way to diagnose endometriosis is to have a pelvic MRI done. *Note: I prefer patients get a pelvic MRI for definitive diagnosis of endometriosis.*

- How to naturally manage symptoms: The truth is, even if you have surgery to remove your endometriosis, without making the lifestyle and dietary changes mapped out for you in this book, the endometriosis will grow right back. The best way to manage endometriosis, even if you don't know you definitely have it but are experiencing many of the above symptoms OR you have some of the symptoms AND you are not conceiving OR you suspect you might have it, is to: follow the fertility-rejuvenation protocol herein and in addition: avoid dairy, pay special attention to your mental–emotional state, and really follow the advice in chapter 7 about letting go of any pent-up emotions, because in Traditional Oriental Medicine (TOM) we often see endometriosis directly linked to repressed emotions.
- What this means for your fertility: Endometriosis cannot only cause hormonal imbalances that can prevent pregnancy but it can also cause anatomical ones, such as blocked fallopian tubes, that can prevent pregnancy. Be disciplined and follow the guide-lines in this book and you will manage your symptoms, regulate your hormones, and improve your fertility. However, keep in mind that the structural damage endometriosis can do to your body, in particular to your fallopian tubes, may require medical interven-tion. But don't feel discouraged as women with endometriosis get pregnant all the time.

OK, now that we have discussed the top three most common fertility issues, how they are linked to autoimmune issues, and how to best manage them, let's discuss the three most common auto-immune diseases. Understanding all of these disease states will empower you to take charge of your health and provide you with crucial information so that you can best rejuvenate your fertility.

The Three Most Commonly Undiagnosed Autoimmune Diseases

Please take the time to look through each of these extremely prev-alent and misdiagnosed fertility-hindering autoimmune diseases, and if you have many matching symptoms, speak to your doctor and follow the specific recommendations I make for each disease.

Most people are misdiagnosed or not diagnosed at all with these diseases and they can have a seriously detrimental effect on your health, your ability to conceive, and your future child:

Type 1 Diabetes

Type 1 diabetes is also known as insulin-dependent diabetes and is a form of diabetes that results from the autoimmune destruction of insulin-producing cells in your pancreas. Insulin is a hormone that regulates carbohydrate and fat metabolism in your body and is responsible for absorbing glucose from the blood. When your insulin is affected your blood sugar is affected, and this causes your hormones to be completely imbalanced, thus resulting in fertility issues.

- Symptoms: Extreme hunger, extreme thirst, frequent urination, weight loss, fatigue. Also, if you experience signs of either hyperglycemia or hypoglycemia, it can be an indicator that you are dealing with insulin and blood sugar issues that can predispose you to type 1 diabetes and PCOS (the most prevalent cause for fertility issues):
  - Hyperglycemia symptoms: Fatigue after meals, must have sweets after meals, frequent urination, increased thirst and appetite, waist girth equal or greater than hip girth, difficulty losing weight.
  - Hypoglycemia symptoms: Eating relieves fatigue; irritabity, get lightheaded, or feels shaky and jittery if meals are missed; agitated easily; poor memory.
- Blood tests you need to ask your doctor to perform:
  - Fasting glucose: should be between 85 and 99 mg/dL
    - A low fasting glucose indicates hypoglycemia; a high one indicates insulin resistance (and likely PCOS).
  - Hemoglobin (HGB) A1C: should be between 4.8% and 5.6%
    - A low HGB A1C indicates hypoglycemia; a high one indicates insulin resistance (and likely PCOS).
  - Total cholesterol: should be between 150 and 199 mg/dL
    - Low cholesterol indicates not enough steroid hormones and can negatively impact fertility; high cholesterol indicates abnormal blood sugar levels (and likely PCOS).
  - Triglycerides: should be between 75 and 100 mg/dL
    - If these are high it indicates blood sugar issues.

○ Low-Density lipoprotein (LDL): should be less than 99 mg/dL
  ■ If this is high it indicates blood sugar issues.
○ High-density lipoprotein (HDL): should be between 55 and 100 mg/dL
  ■ If this is low it indicates a thyroid issue or lack of exercise.
○ Lactase dehydrogenase (LDH): should be between 140 and 180 U/L
  ■ If this is low it indicates hypoglycemia.
○ CO_2: should be between 25 and 300 mmol/L
  ■ If this is low it indicates abnormal blood sugars.
○ Free testosterone: Range can vary between labs; the key here is that if it is high it can indicate both abnormal blood sugars and PCOS.
○ GTT: range can vary depending on test and lab
  ■ If this is low it indicates hypoglycemia; if it is high it indicates insulin resistance (and likely PCOS).

● How to naturally manage symptoms: Follow the fertility-rejuvenation protocol herein, be sure to eat a protein-based breakfast (with 20–30 grams of protein) within the first hour of waking, snack on protein every two to three hours, get in 1 to 2 teaspoons daily of organic fair trade cinnamon, avoid any of the high-sugared fruits we discussed in chapter 5 (eat only one serving per day of low-sugared fruits) and make it a priority to meditate daily.

Cinnamon has been scientifically shown to balance out blood sugar. Add 1 to 2 teaspoons of cinnamon to a mug of hot water and drink daily to help regulate insulin levels.

● What does all of this mean to your fertility: If you are experiencing blood sugar issues regularly, autoimmunity can be triggered, increasing inflammation in your body, causing hormonal imbalances, ovulatory dysfunction, and increased incidence of PCOS. The first step for you is to balance your blood sugar by following the recommendations above (and throughout this book). When your blood sugar stabilizes, so will your hormones.

Autoimmune Thyroid Disease (AITD)

AITD (also known as Hashimoto's or Grave's disease) is when your body's immune system begins attacking its own thyroid gland, resulting in thyroid dysfunction. When the thyroid doesn't function properly, your entire hormonal system is affected, which will negatively impact your fertility.

- Symptoms: AITD can appear with either hypothyroid or hyperthyroid symptoms.
    - Hypothyroid symptoms: Fatigue, sluggishness, cold feet and/or hands, excessive sleeping, easy weight gain, menstrual irregularity (i.e., heavier, more frequent, and more painful periods than you're used to), midcycle spotting, miscarriage, constipation, depression, lack of motivation, morning headaches that wear off as the day progresses, thinning hair or excessive hair loss, dryness of the skin and/or scalp, mental sluggishness.
    - Hyperthyroid symptoms: Heart palpitations, inward trembling, infrequent menses (approximately only 4–5 per year), increased heart rate (even at rest), difficulty gaining weight, high anxiety, hot body temperature, frequent bowel movements, insomnia, night sweats.

My doctor tested my thyroid and it's fine...

It is likely your doctor did not do a *complete* thyroid panel, including testing for thyroid antibodies. Getting your thyroid antibodies tested is imperative to your fertility. Get them tested!

Also, double check your thyroid lab test results with the numbers below to make sure your numbers are in the normal, fertile range.

- Blood tests you need to ask your doctor to do:
    - Thyroid stimulating hormone (TSH): should be between 0.5 and 2.5 mIU/L for optimal fertility and pregnancy
        - If TSH is low it can indicate hyperthyroid, AITD, or too much thyroid medication; if TSH is high it can indicate hypothyroid or AITD. Be sure to have your thyroid antibodies tested.

○ Total T4 (thyroxine): should be between 6.0 and 12.0 µg/dL
  ▪ If T4 is low it can indicate hypothyroidism and low pituitary function; if it is high it can indicate hyperthyroidism.
○ T3 uptake (triiodothyronine): should be between 28% and 36%
  ▪ If T3 uptake is low it indicates too much estrogen (often due to environmental sources such as the birth control pill or beauty products); if T3 uptake is high it indicates too much testosterone (usually due to blood sugar abnormalities).
○ Total T3: should be between 100 and 180 ng/dL
  ▪ If total T3 is low it indicates hypothyroidism; if it is high it indicates hyperthyroidism.
○ Free T4: should be between 0.8 and 1.8 ng/dL
  ▪ If free T4 is low, it indicates hypothyroidism; if it is high it indicates hyperthyroidism.
○ Free T3: should be between 3.0 and 4.0 pg/mL
  ▪ If free T3 is low, it indicates hypothyroidism; if it is high it indicates hyperthyroidism.
○ Thyroid peroxidase antibodies (TPO Ab): These antibodies are present with AITD.
○ Thyroglobulin antibodies (TG Ab): The antibodies are present with AITD.
○ Thyroglobulin stimulating immunoglobulins (TSI): These antibodies are present with AITD.

> If you test positive for any of the thyroid antibodies, you have AITD and need to strictly adhere to the recommendations in this book and be continuously monitored by an endocrinologist. AITD is one of the most overlooked diseases affecting fertility and pregnancy and, especially if you are experiencing any of the above thyroid symptoms, I cannot urge you enough to get your thyroid antibodies tested.

• How to naturally manage symptoms: Follow the fertility-rejuvenation protocol mapped out for you in this book. In addition you must cut out dairy entirely, keep your blood sugar stable (follow the recommendations for managing type 1 diabetes above), get in a handful of selenium-rich brazil nuts daily, and add 5,000 IU per day of vitamin D to your supplement regimen.

- What does this all mean to your fertility: If you are experiencing any of the symptoms of hypothyroidism or hyperthyroidism and having difficulty conceiving or recurring miscarriages, you need to get a complete thyroid panel with thyroid antibodies tested by your doctor. The presence of AITD is significantly higher among women who are having difficulty conceiving, especially those who have endometriosis or ovulation dysfunction.

Dairy, Gluten, and Your Thyroid

If you have AITD you need to stop eating both dairy and gluten. Gliadin (the protein portion of gluten) and casein (the protein portion of cow's milk) both are similarly recognized and attacked by thyroid antibodies. So a body with AITD reacts to dairy, gluten, and thyroid tissue. Removing both dairy and gluten will dramatically improve your health and fertility.

Celiac Disease

Celiac disease (CD) is an autoimmune condition where the body attacks the lining of the small intestine and interferes with the absorption of nutrients from food in response to dietary intake of gluten. Gluten is a protein that is found in many foods such as wheat, rye, and barley (there is more on gluten-containing grains and foods in chapter 5).

- Symptoms: bloating, gas, constipation, diarrhea, itchy skin rash, eczema, psoriasis (also an autoimmune disease), poor weight gain, inability to lose weight, fertility and reproductive disorders, irregular menses, painful cramping with menses, ovulation dysfunction, headaches, depression, irritability, urinary frequency and urgency, body aches and pains, anemia, delayed growth, thinning hair, difficulty healing, brain fog, difficulty concentrating, weak immune system, and thinning bones.
- Tests you need to ask your doctor to do:
  - Celiac antibody blood test for immunoglobulin A (IgA), anti-tissue transglutaminase (tTGA), and IgA anti-endomysium antibodies (AEA). If any of these tests come back elevated, you have CD. *However, if none of these antibodies come up it doesn't*

mean you don't have CD. CD specialist Dr. Kenneth Fine states that blood tests for CD aren't reliable in early stage CD as the antibodies are usually only present in the tissues of the small intestine and not in the blood.

o Endoscopy with a small bowel biopsy: Your doctor will take a sample of tissue from your small intestine. While you are asleep, your doctor passes a long, narrow tube called an endoscope through your mouth and stomach and into the small intestine. The doctor can then remove tissue samples and take photographs. Later, a pathologist will study the tissue samples to check for CD. This is quite an invasive test but is considered to be the most accurate test for CD as long as your doctor gets several samples from your small intestine.

o Stool sample: A laboratory will look at your stool for the presence of the CD antibodies discussed above, as well as for a higher fat content in your stool. Patients with untreated CD (meaning they are still eating gluten) have a difficult time digesting fats and their stool will have a higher fat content than is normal. Some doctors claim the stool sample test is the most accurate way to diagnose CD.

o *Noteworthy*: Many diagnosticians recognize that there are false negatives in the testing of CD (meaning the test comes back negative, saying you don't have it, but you actually do). Therefore, I recommend to my patients to go gluten-free and if your symptoms improve, then although you may not actually have CD, you are having gluten-intolerance issues and your body and your fertility are suffering as a result.

- How to naturally manage symptoms: Follow the plan laid out in this book, be sure to take a double dose of the daily probiotic supplement I recommended in chapter 5, and have one cup of homemade bone broth daily to help heal your intestinal lining.

- What this means for your fertility: If you are experiencing any of the above symptoms of CD on a regular basis *and* you are having difficulty conceiving or having recurring miscarriages, go 100% gluten-free regardless of what your tests show, as you may not have CD but you may be gluten-intolerant and this could be affecting your fertility.

In my practice, the two most commonly undiagnosed autoimmune diseases are CD and AITD. It is estimated by the National Women's Health Information Center that 20 to 30 million individuals—that's 1 in 13 people—have AITD, and half of them are undiagnosed. According to the National Foundation for Celiac Awareness, 1 out of every 133 Americans has CD and 83% of those people are undiagnosed.

Now, to arm you with even more information, let's get into specifics on how TOM breaks down the most common fertility challenges. When you have a grasp of your fertility from both the Western and Eastern views of the symptoms and diagnostics, you will be equipped with the knowledge, and therefore the power, to really shift your fertility and your health.

Fertility Challenges from a TOM Perspective

As this is a book based on TOM principles, I wanted to give you the opportunity here to figure out what your diagnosis is from a TOM perspective. Knowledge is power, so get out your pens or pencils and take a moment to check off which symptoms you commonly experience and then read further to see more specific tips for your individual situation.

Quickly, let's recap the three vital substances that are imperative for optimal fertility:

- *Essence*: Is stored in the kidneys as an energetic reserve, and is considered one of the most vital substances of the human body. It is the basis of our fertility and manages menstrual regularity, ovarian reserve, ovulation, and the thick blood-rich uterine lining. There are two types of essence, prenatal and postnatal essence:
  - *Prenatal essence* is before-birth essence, it is the foundation from which we are created: our genetics passed on from our parents as well as the embryonic environment in which we developed.
  - *Postnatal essence* is after-you've-been-born essence. This is the key to improving fertility. This type of essence is created by how we live our life: diet, exercise, stress management,

emotional balance, and being in touch with nature (as dis-cussed in chapters 2 and 3) all affect our postnatal essence. Postnatal essence affects the quality of our eggs (and the quality of your man's sperm), the quality and thickness of our uterine lining, and the regularity of our menstrual cycle. *Bottom line*: the more of this postnatal essence you can build up, the healthier and more fertile you will be.

- *Qi*: Unlike essence, doesn't reside in one specific organ; rather, it is tied to *all* of our organs. Qi is the "vital energy" that each one of our organs needs to do its job properly. Without Qi there is no life. Qi comes from three sources:
  - The air we breathe
  - The food we eat
  - Our essence
- *Blood*: Is considered the most important liquid substance in our body: it nourishes tissues and organs and its circulation is impera-tive for our bodies to function; it is fundamental for hormonal bal-ance and optimal fertility. In TOM, blood is created from two sources:
  - The food we eat
  - Our essence

Now take your pen or pencil and let's get into this quiz to see how well your essence, Qi, and blood are doing. Go through each column and enter the corresponding letter next to any symptoms you currently experience on a regular basis (one to two times per week *or* with your menstrual cycle each month). Some of you may have symptoms in every category, and that's normal. At the end, we will tally up the letters and I will give you even more specific advice for the symptoms you experience:

Enter an "E" if you experience any of the following symptoms:

Low back pain _____

Hearing problems (such as loss or tinnitus) _____

General body aches and weakness _____

Premature graying of the hair _____

Weak teeth (they break or chip easily) _____

Bone issues (weak or frail and break easily) _____

Feeling cold most of the time, yet hot at night _____

Urinary frequency _____

Poor memory _____

Easily frightened and fearful _____

Lacking confidence _____

Pessimistic and sorrowful _____

Difficulty conceiving _____

Recurring miscarriage _____

Scanty periods (less blood than should be seen, see page 21 for details) _____

Shorter menstrual cycles (typically 24- to 26-day cycles) _____

Little to no fertile cervical mucus _____

Low sex drive _____

A high FSH or low AMH for your age _____

Developmental delays during your childhood _____

Serious childhood illness such as cancer, epilepsy, or diabetes _____

Enter a "Q" if you experience any of the following symptoms:

Poor appetite _____

Nausea _____

Loose stools _____

Undigested food in stool _____

Dull stomach pain _____

Easy sweating without exertion _____

Gas _____

Bloating _____

Foggy brain _____

Feeling cold all the time _____

Craving sweets _____

Fatigue and weakness _____

Difficulty waking in the morning _____

Prolapsed organs _____

Varicose veins _____

Dull achy pain in muscles _____

Easy bruising _____

Hemorrhoids _____

Weak immune system _____

Sinus issues and allergies _____

Obsessive worry _____

Obsessive–compulsive behavior _____

Heavy menstrual bleeding _____

Bleeding or spotting midcycle _____

Recurring miscarriage _____

Feeling of exhaustion with menstruation _____

Premenstrual swelling of breasts and body _____

Aching legs with menstruation _____

Enter an "L" if you experience any of the following symptoms:
Pain along the sides of your body or in your rib cage area
_____

Alternating diarrhea and constipation _____

Tense neck and shoulders _____

Frequent sighing _____

Hiccups _____

A feeling of a lump in your throat _____

Mood swings _____

Bitter taste in your mouth _____

Churning sensation in your stomach _____

Irritability _____

Frustration _____

Anger _____

Rage _____

Depression _____

Tendency toward repressing emotions _____

Intense PMS with sore breasts _____

Painful cramping with your period _____

Diarrhea with your period _____

Breakouts on your chin premenstrually _____

Enter a "B" if you experience any of the following symptoms:

Palpitations _____

Dizziness _____

Insomnia _____

Fatigue (especially after your period or with exercise) _____

Shortness of breath _____

Dream-disturbed sleep _____

Easily startled _____

Poor memory _____

Poor concentration _____

Dull pale complexion _____

Anemia _____

Pale lips _____

Always cold _____

Muscle cramps _____

Numbness and tingling (especially in hands and feet) _____

Headaches that feel better with pressure _____

Dry hair _____

Blurred vision or floaters _____

Dry and/or brittle nails _____

Thinning hair _____

Knee pain _____

Irritability _____

Mild depression _____

Anxiety _____

Guilt _____

Scanty or little to no menstrual blood that is pale to light pink in color _____

Increased anxiety premenstrually _____

Night sweats premenstrually _____

Low libido _____

Thin uterine lining _____

Enter an "S" if you experience any of the following symptoms:

Painful, fixed masses, typically in the abdomen _____

Abdominal pain _____

Purple nails _____

Purple lips _____

A dark complexion _____

Dark circles around the eyes _____

Fixed pain in other areas of the body (such as the head or the upper back) _____

Jaw-clenching/ teeth-grinding _____

Depression (can be severe) _____

Anger _____

Rage _____

Extreme emotional swings _____

Deeply repressed emotions _____

Pessimism _____

Self-deprecating thoughts _____

A very low self-esteem _____

Heavy, dark, clotty, and painful menstrual cycles _____

Fibrocystic breasts _____

Uterine fibroids _____

OK, now take a moment and tally up your letters. If you have 8 to 10 or more symptoms in one of the above columns, then you need to read up on the category of symptoms you most experience and start applying some of the additional tips below.

- *E stands for essence* and how it relates to essence deficiency. If you have 8 to 10 or more of the "E" symptoms, please read the essence section below.
- *Q stands for Qi* and how it relates to Qi deficiency. If you have 8 to 10 or more of the "Q" symptoms, please read the Qi deficiency section below.
- *L stands for liver* and how it relates to liver Qi stagnation. If you have 8 to 10 or more of the "L" symptoms, please read the liver Qi stagnation section below.
- *B stands for blood* and how it relates to blood deficiency. If you have 8 to 10 or more of the "B" symptoms, please read the blood section below.
- *S stands for stagnation* and how it relates to blood stagnation. If you have 8 to 10 or more of the "S" symptoms, please read the blood stagnation section below.

Essence and Fertility Challenges

Essence is imperative to optimal health and fertility. Essence deficiency means that your body may not have enough essence to be able to get pregnant and carry that pregnancy to term. Whether that deficiency is of prenatal or postnatal nature, the TOM approach is the same: to nourish and build essence, for without essence, QI, and blood cannot flourish and fertility cannot be rejuvenated. Keep in mind: all of the most common Western medical reasons for fertility issues have some essence-deficiency symptoms in common.

How to improve your essence: this entire book is about nourishing your essence so follow *all* of the advice, especially about drinking bone broth daily (mentioned in chapter 6) and about boosting your confidence and courage (in chapter 7). In addition, incorporate these essence-building superfoods into your life:

- Royal jelly promotes longevity and reproductive ability in the queen bee, and can impart those same attributes to humans. It is rich in amino acids, lipids, sugars, vitamins, and most importantly, proteins. It contains high levels of vitamins D and E, and also has ample levels of iron and calcium. Take one to two teaspoons in lukewarm (not hot) water daily. A reputable brand is YS Organic Bee Farms (http://www.ysorganic.com/index.html). *If you have a bee allergy, do NOT take royal jelly.*

> Since bees seem to be rapidly declining, be sure to choose high-quality royal jelly from a reputable, organic, free-range, biodynamic farming and bee-keeping source.

- Cordyceps is a widely used Chinese herb (it's actually a fungus) that boosts the immune system, promotes vitality, nourishes essence, reduces the signs of aging, and enhances libido. Take 1200 mg per day. Kan Herb Company makes a great cordyceps product.
- Caviar goes by many names such as tobiko, fish roe, and ikura, and is a fertility superfood that is loaded with fertility and Qi-enhancing omega-3 fatty acids. Eat 1 ounce one to two times per week.

Qi Deficiency and Fertility Issues

Qi deficiency means there is not enough Qi in your body to circulate to your organs to help them function properly, and your health, vitality, and fertility all suffer. Qi deficiency commonly affects women. For optimal fertility, we need sufficient amounts of Qi so that all our organs can get the nourishment they need to remain healthy and fertile.

How to boost your body's Qi: the best thing to do is to strictly adhere to the *Yes, You Can Get Pregnant* diet, as abundant Qi comes from the foods you eat. Also, keep in mind that fertility patients with Qi deficiency do best when they avoid dairy (in addition to gluten, soy, and sugar) and eat small meals regularly throughout the day. Be sure to take a daily probiotic (as mentioned in chapter 5). In addition, incorporate these Qi-boosting lifestyle modifications into your daily life:

- Eat only cooked or lightly steamed foods: the spleen likes to be warm, and eating too many cold, raw foods will further weaken your spleen Qi.
- Meditate: this is really important for the overthinking spleen Qi person. Taking some time away from worrying will help boost your Qi (refresh your memory on how to meditate in chapter 4).
- Each morning, sip a mug of hot water with sliced ginger, a half teaspoon of powdered cinnamon, the juice from half a lemon and a half teaspoon of raw, organic honey. This warming elixir will help tonify your spleen and improve your digestion.

Liver Qi Stagnation and Fertility Issues

Qi stagnation means there is likely (but not always) enough Qi in your body, but it's stuck or blocked somewhere. When liver Qi stagnation arises, the Qi is not flowing smoothly through your body and symptoms such as those mentioned above arise. Liver Qi stagnation is often a result of long-term emotional repression.

To get your liver Qi moving, incorporate the following into your daily routine: Be super strict about removing all environmental toxins and endocrine-disrupting chemicals from your lifestyle as these noxious substances clog up the liver and further stagnate it (more on this in chapter 6), follow the *Yes, You Can Get Pregnant* diet, and be sure to practice all of the recommendations in chapter 7. These exercises are important for everyone, but especially for you, as most of your stagnation comes from an emotional source. In addition, be sure to:

- Exercise daily. Your stagnant liver Qi longs to be moved; 30 to 45 minutes per day of moderate cardio will feel so good to you.

- Express your emotions. Stop keeping things in. Even if it's expressing yourself in a letter you will never send, get out the pent up emotions inside of you.
- Meditate with deep, deeeeep breathing. The act of deep inhalation and long exhalation helps move the liver Qi and unblock you. I want you to focus on sending yourself love. With liver diseases in TOM there is a strong emotional component of "self attacking self." During your meditation send yourself love; you deserve it.
- Begin each day with a mug of hot water, squeeze the juice from one full lemon, add a teaspoon of apple cider vinegar, and drink. The sour nature of this beverage will help move your stuck liver Qi.

Blood Deficiency and Your Fertility

Blood deficiency means that there is not enough blood in your body to nourish your tissues and organs. When it comes to fertility, blood is extremely important for the overall health of your uterus and entire reproductive system, including your uterine lining and growing follicles.

To nourish and tone your blood, it is important that you eat enough protein, especially animal protein, and follow the *Yes, You Can Get Pregnant* diet. Be sure to focus on eating liver (or take liver pills, as recommended in chapter 5) and meditate daily to manage anxiety.Here are some tips to help balance your heart blood:

- Take a tablespoon of organic, unsulphured blackstrap molasses daily. Molasses is extremely rich in B vitamins and will help nourish your blood.
- Be strict about having four almonds or a half-cup of unsweetened almond milk right before bed. This will help keep your blood sugar even while you sleep and encourage your body to sleep more soundly.
- Do more yoga and less cardio. Too much cardiovascular exercise will burn up your liver blood. You will benefit from more gentle exercise such as yoga and pilates.

- Be easy on yourself. We say in TOM that our liver blood can get depleted by constant emotional harassment, or as I said earlier in this chapter, by "self attacking self." Take time each day and write down five reasons why you love YOU.

Blood Stagnation and Your Fertility

Blood stagnation means that blood is literally stuck. When blood is stuck it pools, it blocks, and it inhibits healthy circulation throughout your entire body and is especially detrimental to your fertility. Usually, blood stagnation is a result of liver Qi stagnation. Blood stagnation is closely related to the symptoms and presentation of endometriosis.

To get your blood circulating again it is important to follow the dietary and lifestyle recommendations made throughout this book, but for you, the emotional work is your biggest task. Digging deep and releasing pent-up emotions will help the most, and for that I not only encourage the work I give you in this book but also that you seek out professional psychological help. In addition, be sure to:

- Take a baby aspirin each day as this helps to thin your blood and will assist in resolving menstrual and fertility difficulties. Use caution and speak with your doctor if you are on any other medications.
- Do a daily castor oil pack on your lower abdomen. Apply a thin layer of castor oil over your lower abdomen (the area below your belly button), cover with one sheet of saran wrap, and on top of the saran wrap place a hot water bottle. Sit with the castor oil pack on for 20 minutes. This will help break up abdominal and uterine masses.
- Get Mayan abdominal massage regularly. Mayan abdominal massage is an invigorating abdominal massage practiced by trained practitioners. Go to: https://arvigotherapy.com for more information and to find a practitioner near you.

We have just covered the most common fertility challenges, from an Eastern and Western perspective and offered you some great tips that you can start doing today to manage them. As with all fertility challenges, a multifaceted approach like the one outlined in this book is the best method to improve your health and your fertility. Don't just do the diet portion and ignore the other recommendations. Remember your mantra: *I have the power to change MY health and improve MY fertility*, and know that your power lies in applying, living, and owning *all* of the advice in this book.

Turn the page and check out what top reproductive endocrinologists had to say when I asked them some very specific questions relating to your fertility.

11
Getting Inside the Head of Your Doctor: Top Reproductive Endocrinologists Speak

Over the past 10 years, I have treated hundreds of women who were trying to conceive. I feel beyond thankful in saying that I have helped most all of them achieve their dream of becoming a mother. However, I should also add that many of these women were not only under my care, but also under the care of outstanding reproductive endocrinologists at top fertility clinics. I do strongly believe in the power of Traditional Oriental Medicine (TOM) and in the fertility rejuvenation protocol laid out in this book, but I must add: I believe that Western medical fertility treatments are powerful too. For some women, it is the combined approach of Western and Eastern medicine that helps them get pregnant. To best empower you on this fertility-rejuvenating journey, I spoke with top reproductive endocrinologists to get their opinion on fertility.

❄

Dr. Hugh Taylor, a board certified specialist in obstetrics and gynecology and in reproductive endocrinology, as well as the chair of the Department of Obstetrics Gynecology, and Reproductive Sciences at the Yale School of Medicine, the Chief of Obstetrics and Gynecology at Yale-New Haven Hospital, and the director of the Yale Center for Reproductive Biology, spoke with me at length over such topics as epigenetics, autoimmune diseases, mind–body medicine, and egg freezing. Here's what he had to say:

Aimee Raupp: *How do you see epigenetics affecting fertility?*

Dr. Hugh Taylor: *Epigenetics is a huge issue, it is not well understood. Clearly [epigenetics] is having an impact on fertility. Science shows that fetal exposures (meaning exposures that your mother had to environmental agents/endocrine–disrupting chemicals while she was pregnant with you) clearly impact women in their fertile years.*

Aimee Raupp: *Can exposure to environmental agents/endocrine–disrupting chemicals affect a women's fertility later in life?*

Dr. Hugh Taylor: *These influences can impact fertility; the earlier in development the exposure, the greater the risk. Environmental agents are clearly leading to infertility. When it comes to PCOS and endometriosis there is no clear genetic cause. You can inherit a propensity to develop PCOS or endometriosis; however, heredity alone is not enough. These diseases result from a complex interplay between genetic risk, developmental programming, and environmental cues.*

Aimee Raupp: *With nearly 30% of fertility issues being diagnosed as "idiopathic," do you think the majority of these idiopathic cases are actually misdiagnosed or are undiagnosed autoimmune conditions?*

Dr. Hugh Taylor: *Some idiopathic cases are autoimmune, but not all of them. When it comes to infertility there is so much more that we don't understand than we do. Impacts from autoimmune diseases, environmental triggers, damage from other diseases, all play a role in ovarian aging and infertility.*

Aimee Raupp: *Do you think age is our biggest fertility issue?*

Dr. Hugh Taylor: *Age is certainly not the biggest issue. It is a large issue and women need to be made aware of how their fertility changes with age.*

Aimee Raupp: *What are your thoughts on egg freezing? If you had a friend who was over 35 and single, would you recommend she freeze her eggs?*

Dr. Hugh Taylor: *Yes, I would.*

Aimee Raupp: *But isn't it true that frozen embryos are much more stable than frozen eggs when thawing?*

Dr. Hugh Taylor: *Yes. But egg freezing techniques are getting better and better. When freezing eggs for future use, you need more eggs than if you are using embryos; however, to create an embryo we need sperm. Some may not be at a point in life where they are ready to commit to use a partner's or donor's sperm.*

Aimee Raupp: *Say that same woman in a few years winds up needing to do an IVF. Would you use her frozen eggs or fresh eggs to do the IVF?*

Dr. Hugh Taylor: *I always prefer fresh over frozen. However, if aging has left her without strong eggs, the frozen eggs will solve the problem.*

Aimee Raupp: *What do you think about the difference between chronological age and physiological age? Do you ever think about that?*

Dr. Hugh Taylor: *Yes, you bring up a good point. There is so much variability as to when someone's ovaries start to fail. Yes, chronological age is a good estimate, but it doesn't really tell us what we want to know...when we start combining chronological age with AMH [anti-Müllerian hormone] or FSH [follicule-stimulating hormone] we can get a better idea. But we do need a better formula to come up with to determine a women's physiological age, as you put it, and that may be the key to not only how a woman will respond to an IVF treatment but also counseling women about planning for a family. Aging varies from person to person, and we know that there are environmental and genetic influences. Certainly smoking and all sorts of other environmental agents that we don't yet fully understand yet are limiting our reproductive life span.*

Aimee Raupp: *Is FSH a static number (meaning it stays the same)? And do you use FSH or AMH to determine ovarian reserve?*

Dr. Hugh Taylor: *FSH is not static. We look at AMH and FSH, but AMH is more stable. We want to see an AMH over 1.*

Aimee Raupp: *I know more and more fertility clinics are now recommending certain supplements to their patients to help improve egg quality. What are your thoughts on this?*

Dr. Hugh Taylor: *I don't necessarily advocate for the use of supplements, but I don't see them as harmful. As of yet, there isn't solid evidence saying they help improve egg quality...the notion that they can improve egg quality is interesting and promising, and I don't think there's any harm in it. I'm not against it.*

Aimee Raupp: *Do you recommend meditation or other stress–relieving techniques to your patients?*

Dr. Hugh Taylor: *Yes. It's important for the patient to be proactive, involved, and working to alleviate stress. Meditation or anything that reduces stress levels is going to help.*

Aimee Raupp: *Do you recommend acupuncture to your patients?*

Dr. Hugh Taylor: *It is hard to determine (scientifically) the benefit of acupuncture, as it is hard to control in scientific experiments. I do think it is a good idea for the right woman who is open to it. Certainly, there are women who are invested in it and benefit from it.*

Aimee Raupp: *What are your thoughts on celiac disease (CD) and fertility?*

Dr. Hugh Taylor: *The science is there: there is a clear link between CD and infertility. It is something we rule out in all of our fertility patients.*

My big takeaway from my interview with Dr. Taylor was his statement, "There is so much more about infertility we don't know than we do." Of course, there is plenty of data suggesting that advanced maternal age is playing a role in fertility, but as he said, "age is certainly not the biggest issue." Yes, age is a large issue and one that women need to be aware of; however, the conversation I had with Dr. Taylor focused much more on environmental influences, endocrine–disrupting chemicals, and epigenetics, and how these factors are affecting our fertility. Dr. Taylor's current research mainly focuses upon environmental agents and how they are epigenetically affecting us reproductively. During our conversation, he also shared with me his curiosity about how genetically modified foods may also be affecting our reproductive capabilities. All in all, I was inspired by his passion for helping women to find the right solutions or help them get pregnant. And I felt I gained insight into the future of reproductive medical research: how our environment—our diet, our stress levels, the products we use on our bodies, and the chemicals we are exposed to throughout our entire lives—is affecting our fertility.

✳

Dr. Janelle Luk is a board certified specialist in obstetrics and gynecology and in reproductive endocrinology, as well as the co-director of the Diminished Ovarian Reserve Program at New Hope Fertility Center in New York City. She is an innovator in her field, employing a combination of conventional stimulation methods (meaning using pharmaceutical medications) and the natural cycle stimulation protocol (meaning no medications) to synthesize the most optimal stimulation method for each individual patient. Dr. Luk and I discussed topics from can a woman safely wait to her 40s to get pregnant to what type of dietary recommendations she thinks are best for fertility patients. Here is what she had to say:

Aimee Raupp: *From your clinical perspective, do you believe a woman can safely wait until she's 40 to try to get pregnant?*

Dr. Janelle Luk: *From my clinical perspective, I believe that a woman should not wait until 40 years old to try to get pregnant. First of all, everyone's biological clock is different. However, starting from a patient's earlier age, there is already a gradual decrease in ovarian reserve. But at the age of 35 and older, the decrease is more clinically significant. As a result, I would suggest that trying earlier than 40 years of age is better.*

Aimee Raupp: *From your clinical perspective, do you feel women should go to IVF (in vitro fertilization) over doing multiple IUIs [intrauterine inseminations]?*

Dr. Janelle Luk: *That really depends on the patient's tubal patency (meaning how open their fallopian tubes are) and also the patient's age. I have told my patients that they are ultimately the ones who need to make that decision. However, I would provide them with utmost guidance in the hope that we could find a timetable that would fit their needs to reach their ultimate goal. For example, if a patient is older than 40 years old and had tried timed intercourse for two years with normal semen analysis, then I would have the patient try IUI, maybe for two months (only if insurance covers it) and then transition to IVF. I would not have a patient try IUI for too long.*

Aimee Raupp: *What's your take on natural IVFs? For what population do you think this approach would be best?*

Dr. Janelle Luk: *My take on natural IVF is that the patient has to be well informed in what she is getting into and it has to be selective. Patients who have had a hypersensitivity with any ovulation induction medications, who have premature ovarian failure and extreme diminished ovarian reserve, will be ideal for natural IVF cycles.*

Aimee Raupp: *What is your take on preimplantation genetic diagnosis (PGD)? Are you at all concerned about how PGD can affect embryonic development?*

Dr. Janelle Luk: *Our center is publishing our own PGD data in this coming year where we have found that PGD has significantly improved the implantation rate/pregnancy rate/live birth rate of embryos that have normal genetic make-up. I believe that PGD is the future of IVF. It has the highest success rate and is a very precise and accurate answer for some patients.*

Aimee Raupp: *Do you find acupuncture to be effective for your patients?*

Dr. Janelle Luk: *Yes, but only when the patient finds a good match. I think that it is very important to find an acupuncturist who is compatible with the patient.*

Aimee Raupp: *Do you ever recommend meditation to your patients? Or any other forms of stress reduction? If so, which ones?*

Dr. Janelle Luk: *Yes, I recommend that patients do exercise, talk to friends, and join forums to discuss their experience. It is a stressful process and sometimes can be a long journey. So it is crucial with alternative therapy to have a good support system.*

Aimee Raupp: *Do you believe follicle–stimulating hormone (FSH) or anti-Müllerian hormone (AMH) to be static numbers? Which (FSH or AMH) do you feel is a better indicator of ovarian reserve?*

Dr. Janelle Luk: *FSH is not a static number. AMH is more of a static number. They are numbers that reflect the ovarian reserve. However, when one is treating a patient, one is not treating only the numbers. It is a good indicator, but you also have to take care of the patient as a whole. Factors such as a patient's menstrual cycle length, ovary sizes, and antral follicle count are all indicators of ovarian reserve.*

Aimee Raupp: *Do you ever make nutritional or lifestyle recommendations to your patients? If so, what are they?*

Dr. Janelle Luk: *I love an antioxidant diet. I have patients who claim that it has worked for them (to improve egg quality). However, I also know that it has not been proven that there is a fertility diet that works for a specific person or population. So this is really patient–dependent. In general, it is important to eat more vegetables than meat.*

❄

Dr. Luk offered me some additional insight, similarly to Dr. Taylor, into how uncertain Western medical science is in predicting fertility for women, regardless of their age. As Dr. Luk said, "When one is treating a patient, one is not only treating numbers ... but you also have to take care of the patient as a whole." Again, age is big determinant in both Dr. Luk's and Dr. Taylor's treatment of their patients—as is the case with most all Western medically trained fertility specialists—however, Dr. Luk and Dr. Taylor both do recognize that age is not the biggest issue and that ovarian aging is dependent upon many concomitant factors. What I also love about Dr. Luk's approach is that she recognizes the importance of antioxidants and diet in the health of her fertility patients.

These interviews helped me gauge where the current fertility research is focused and how multifactorial this whole fertility "epidemic" is. Fertility is not just dependent upon a woman's age, nor on her FSH or AMH levels, but it is also a combination of many factors—lifestyle, diet, stress levels, mental–emotional states, environmental toxins, previous or concurring illnesses, the patient's overall state of health, and the emotional support she has in her life. The fertility–rejuvenation plan outlined in this book will help you address all of these factors and will most definitely improve your fertility and your health. Whether you get pregnant naturally or with assistance from Western medical specialists like Dr. Taylor or Dr. Luk—following the *Yes, You Can Get Pregnant* protocol and being in an optimal state of physical and mental–emotional health when you get pregnant is the best thing we can do for our future generations.

Afterword

You Are Where You're Supposed to Be

I want to sincerely thank YOU for taking the time to read this book and for allowing me to come along on this fertility-rejuvenating journey with you. We covered a lot of information and I am excited for you to take it all in and begin your self-love health mission lifestyle overhaul.

You now know how *my least favorite word*, the one you're not to use any more, is hurting your heart and your uterus and your ability to get pregnant.

You're clear on how your fertile body works, when the best time to try to conceive is, and how important orgasms are in conception.

You're aware of how your lifestyle choices are affecting your epigenetics and your essence and ultimately your health and your fertility.

You've committed to the *Yes, You Can Get Pregnant* fertility-rejuvenation plan and are becoming one with nature, eating for optimal nutrition and egg quality, steering clear of environmental toxins, and preparing yourself mentally and emotionally so that you can become the mother you want to be.

You are excited about meditating daily and saying your mantras because both are so good for your overall health.

You have the fertility rejuvenation roadmap that you can and will follow with effortless ease.

You are already feeling more healthy and vibrant and eager for your health and fertility to only get better.

You feel empowered by all the knowledge you now possess and are ready to take the next steps toward reclaiming your health and your fertility.

You love your new mantra: *I have the power to improve MY health and MY fertility*. You believe in that mantra. You own it. And I, too, believe in that mantra for you. I know you can take back the power and rejuvenate your health and your fertility.

There's one last thing I want to discuss before this book ends: the importance of embracing that you are always where you are supposed to be. By this I mean, life is a series of steps, one following the next, and you are on your path. Accept your path. Don't fight it. Rather, take it with stride, appreciate where you are, and know that where you are headed is better than where you've been before. You are always where you're supposed to be.

Sometimes your path will feel tumultuous and unclear and other times it will be flourishing and peaceful. No matter where you find yourself: embrace it and know that better things are on their way to you. Know that you deserve all that you desire. Know that your life is unfolding precisely as it should and that *right here, right now* is where you're supposed to be. Keep seeing the vision of where you want to be (your mindful daydreaming tool is the best way to do this) and feel the feeling of that vision: see it, feel it, know it, meditate on it *daily*. Take all the information in this book and own it, let it become you, and honor the self-love health mission your fertile body longs to be on.

One day at a time, with constant appreciation, gratitude, and self-love you will follow the *Yes, You Can Get Pregnant* fertility-rejuvenation protocol and you *will* improve your health and your fertility. You have the power, now run with it!

All my love and gratitude,

XO

Aimee

Resources

Aimee Approved Products

At the time I made this list, the products mentioned contain "Aimee Approved" ingredients. However, companies change formulations all the time, so when it comes to beauty, body, and household products, always check out the rating of your chosen product on the Environmental Working Group's Skin Deep Cosmetic Database (www.ewg.org/skindeep/). It's my go-to for any product!

And, when it comes to gluten-free food, read ingredients and watch out for added sugar, soy, GMO corn, and any ingredients that sound like chemicals. Eat foods as close to their natural state as possible, all the time.

Gluten-Free Products

Crackers: *Edward & Sons, Mary's Gone Crackers*
Pasta: *Andean Dream*
Bread: *Udi's*
Oatmeal: *Bob's Red Mill*
Granola: *Purely Elizabeth*
Cold Cereal: *Arrowhead Mill's*

On-the-Go Snacks

Health bars: *Lärabars* and *Go Raw Bars*
Artisana Nut Butter or coconut butter packets

Body and Beauty Products

Shampoo: *Soap for Goodness Sake Shampoo and Body Bar, California Baby Shampoo, Aubrey Organics*

Body lotion: *L'Occitane Shea Butter, Soap for Goodness Sake Cocoa Butter*

Toothpaste: *Weleda Salt, Redmond Earthpaste, Jack and Jill Organic*

Soap: *Dr. Bronner's, Aubrey Organics, Badger*

Body wash: *Dr. Bronner's 18-in-1 Hemp Pure Castile Soap, Kiss My Face Peace Soap, Terra Firma Cosmetics: A Girl's Gotta Wash*

Facial cleanser: *Badger Rose Geranium Face & Body Soap, Bare Organics All-in-One Cleanser*

Moisturizer: *Badger Facial Oil, Evanhealy Facial Serum*

Make up: *Josie Maran, 100% Pure, Suki, bareMinerals, Modern Minerals, Jane Iredale, Rejuva, Herbal Choice*

To find out more about my own line of beauty products, visit www.YesICanGetPregant.com. Items include:

Body lotion: *Aimee Raupp Beauty Body Butter*

Facial cleanser: *Aimee Raupp Beauty Organic Argan Oil Facial Cleanser*

Moisturizer: *Aimee Raupp Beauty Facial Oils*

Household Cleaning Supplies

Laundry products: *The Good Home Co., Green Shield Organics, Arm & Hammer Super Washing Soda Detergent*

All-purpose household cleaners: *Aussan Natural, Attitude*

A Note About Some Popular Green Household Brands: Popular brands like *Ecover, Method, Seventh Generation,* and *Mrs. Meyer's,* although eco-friendly and sustainably

(continued)

(continued)

manufactured, distribute products that contain some harsh chemicals such as sodium lauryl sulfate and fragrance or parfum.

Bottom line: read ingredients and be conscious of what hidden chemicals are in popular brands. Even if they seem "clean," they may not be.

Do-It-Yourself

This is my go-to method of cleaning:

Baking soda works well for scrubbing counters, tubs, and sinks.
Vinegar and water solution (mixed 50/50) easily cleans windows and mirrors without leaving streaks.
Olive oil mixed with lemon juice (mixed 50/50) can be used as furniture polish.
Tea tree oil diluted with water works to remove mold (1 part tea tree oil to 5 parts water).

As new products are always coming out, be sure to check out www.YesICanGetPregnant.com for more "Aimee Approved" products and recommendations.

Recipes

Here are some of my favorite, super easy, and delicious recipes for you to incorporate into your *Yes I Can Get Pregnant* self-love health mission. Enjoy!

Bone Broth Recipes (adapted from *Nourishing Traditions* by Sally Fallon)

Here are three different bone broth recipes. The chicken stock is my favorite. For those of you who prefer to eat fish rather than meat, the fish stock recipe is easy to make as well. Enjoy!

Chicken Stock

1 whole free-range chicken* or 2 to 3 pounds of bony chicken parts, such as necks, backs, breastbones, and wings

Gizzards from one chicken (*optional*)

2 to 4 chicken feet (*optional*)

4 quarts cold, filtered water

2 tablespoons vinegar

1 large onion, coarsely chopped

2 carrots, peeled and coarsely chopped

3 celery stalks, coarsely chopped

1 bunch parsley

Note: Farm-raised, free-range chickens give the best results.

1. If you are using a whole chicken, remove the fat glands and gizzards from the cavity. Remove the neck and wings and cut them into several pieces.
2. Place whole chicken and chopped-up neck and wings or chicken pieces in a large stainless steel pot with water, vinegar, and all vegetables except parsley.
3. Let stand 30 to 60 minutes.
4. Bring to a boil, removing scum that rises to the top. Reduce heat, cover, and simmer for six to eight hours. The longer you cook the stock, the richer and more flavorful it will be. About 10 minutes before finishing the stock, add parsley. This will impart additional mineral ions to the broth.
5. Remove whole chicken and/or pieces/bones with a slotted spoon; discard the bones. If you are using a whole chicken, let cool and remove chicken meat from the carcass. Reserve for other uses, such as chicken salads, enchiladas, sandwiches, or curries.
6. Strain the stock into a large bowl; discard residue. Reserve the liquid in your refrigerator until the fat rises to the top and congeals. Skim off this fat and reserve the stock in covered containers in your refrigerator or freezer.

Beef Stock

4 pounds beef marrow and knuckle bones (from grass-fed beef)

1 calf's foot, cut into pieces (*optional*)

3 pounds meaty rib or neck bones

4 or more quarts cold, filtered water

½ cup vinegar

3 onions, coarsely chopped

3 carrots, coarsely chopped

3 celery stalks, coarsely chopped

Several sprigs of fresh thyme, tied together

1 teaspoon dried green peppercorns, crushed

1 bunch parsley

1. Preheat oven to 350°F.
2. Place the knuckle and marrow bones and calf's foot in a very large pot with vinegar, and cover with water. Let stand for one hour.
3. Meanwhile, place the meaty bones in a roasting pan and brown in the oven. When well-browned, add to the pot.
4. Pour the fat out of the roasting pan, add cold water to the pan, set over a high flame on the stovetop, and bring to a boil, stirring with a wooden spoon to loosen up coagulated juices. Add this liquid to the pot.
5. Add all vegetables, thyme, and peppercorns to the pot. Add additional water, if necessary, to cover the bones, but the liquid should come no higher than within 1 inch of the rim of the pot, as the volume expands slightly during cooking.
6. Bring to a boil. A large amount of scum will come to the top, and it is important to remove this with a spoon. After you have skimmed, reduce heat and add the thyme and crushed peppercorns.
7. Simmer stock for at least 12 and as long as 72 hours (if it is feasible and in good judgement). Just before finishing, add the parsley and simmer another 10 minutes.
8. Remove bones with tongs or a slotted spoon; discard. Strain the stock into a large bowl; discard residue. Let cool in the refrigerator and remove the congealed fat that rises to the top. Transfer to smaller containers and to the freezer for long-term storage.

Fish Stock

Ideally, fish stock is made from the bones of sole or turbot. In Europe, you can buy these fish on the bone. The fishmonger skins and filets the fish for you, giving you the filets for your evening meal and the bones for making the stock and final sauce. Unfortunately, in America sole arrives at the fish market preboned. But snapper, rock fish, and other non-oily fish work equally well; and a good fish merchant will save the carcasses for you if you ask him. As he normally throws these carcasses away, he shouldn't charge you for them. Be sure to take the heads as well as the body—these are especially rich in iodine and fat-soluble vitamins. Classic cooking texts advise against using oily fish such as salmon for making broth, probably because highly unsaturated fish oils become rancid during the long cooking process.

3 or 4 whole carcasses, including heads, of nonoily fish such as sole, turbot, rockfish, or snapper

About 3 quarts cold, filtered water

2 tablespoons butter

2 onions, coarsely chopped

1 carrot, coarsely chopped

Several sprigs fresh thyme, tied together

Several sprigs parsley

1 bay leaf

½ cup dry white wine or vermouth

¼ cup vinegar

1. Melt butter in a large stainless steel pot. Add the vegetables and cook very gently, about 30 minutes, until they are soft.
2. Add wine and bring to a boil.
3. Add the fish carcasses and cover with cold filtered water. Add vinegar. Tie herbs together and add to the pot. Bring to a boil and skim off the scum and impurities as they rise to the top.
4. Reduce heat, cover, and simmer for at least 4 hours or as long as 24 hours. Remove carcasses with tongs or a slotted spoon and discard. Strain the liquid into pint-sized storage containers for refrigerator or freezer; discard residue. Chill well in the refrigerator and remove any congealed fat before transferring to the freezer for long-term storage.

Aimee's Famous Guacamole

2 avocados, cut into ¼-inch cubes

1 tomato

¼ of a red onion

2 cloves garlic, finely chopped

2 dashes balsamic vinegar

Juice from ½ a lemon

In a large bowl, using a fork, mash all the ingredients together. That's it!

Homemade Health Bars

Raw Walnut Bars (makes 8 to 10 bars)

2 cups raw walnuts

1 cup pitted dates

¼ cup dried cranberries

1 tablespoon cocoa powder

1 teaspoon coconut oil

½ teaspoon sea salt

1. Place all ingredients in a food processor and puree until smooth.
2. Shape puree into 4- to 6-ounce bars.
3. Store in a BPA-free Tupperware® container or glass container.

Coconut Date Bars (makes 8 to 10 bars)

1 cup of almonds

1 cup of cashews

1 cup pitted dates

½ cup shredded coconut (unsweetened)

1 teaspoon coconut oil

1. Place all ingredients in a food processor and puree until smooth.
2. Form into 4- to 6-ounce bars.
3. Store in a BPA-free Tupperware® container or glass container.

Hummus

3 cups drained cooked organic chickpeas (you can use canned organic chickpeas in BPA-free cans)

2 medium cloves garlic

¼ teaspoon crushed red pepper (*optional*)

½ cup tahini

2 tablespoons cold, filtered water

4 tablespoons organic lemon juice, to taste

4 tablespoons organic extra-virgin olive oil

1 tablespoons chopped parsley leaves

¼ teaspoon paprika

1. In a food processor, puree the chickpeas, garlic cloves, red pepper, tahini, water, half the lemon juice, and half the olive oil until smooth, stopping to scrape down the sides as needed. Taste and adjust the seasoning by adding salt and additional lemon juice, if necessary, to your liking.
2. Transfer to a wide shallow bowl for serving and use the back of a serving spoon to form a well in the center of the hummus. Drizzle with the remaining olive oil and sprinkle the top with the parsley and paprika.

Kale Chips

1 bunch of kale, washed and dried

3 tablespoons of melted coconut oil

Salt to taste

1. Preheat oven to 300°F.
2. Remove center stems from the kale and either tear or cut up the leaves.
3. Toss the kale and coconut oil together in a large bowl; sprinkle with salt.
4. Spread on a baking sheet (or two, depending on the amount of kale). Bake for 15 minutes or until crisp.

Liver Pâté

½ lb chicken livers (or beef) (free-range/grass-fed)

1 clove garlic, minced

3 thick slices of organic bacon, chopped in cubes

1 large diced onion

¾ cup butter

4 tablespoons chopped parsley

3 tablespoons sherry (or vinegar)

Fresh nutmeg (*optional*)

Salt and pepper, to taste

1. Heat a large pan to medium high heat and cook the bacon for about three minutes.
2. Add the onion, garlic, and a quarter-cup of the butter and soften for another three or four minutes.
3. Prepare the livers by cutting out the white stringy part. Add the livers to the pan and cook for about 7 to 10 minutes with a little more of the butter.
4. Once cooked through, add sherry, parsley, and salt, pepper, and fresh nutmeg to taste.
5. Remove from heat and pour mixture into a blender or food processor and blend until smooth. Pour the smooth mixture into a serving dish.
6. Melt the remaining butter and pour over the pâté evenly. Cover and put in the refrigerator to cool until the fat hardens.

Enjoy as a snack on celery sticks, on lettuce leaves, or directly off the spoon since it's so good on its own.

Shrimp Salad

3 eggs, hard boiled, peeled, and chopped

2 cups cooked and peeled shrimp, chopped

1 green apple, cored and diced

½ red onion, diced

4 stalks of celery, diced

¼ cup ground Dijon mustard

2 tablespoons white wine vinegar

1 tablespoon olive oil

1 tablespoon raw honey (*optional*)

½ teaspoon parsley (fresh is best)

½ teaspoon thyme (fresh is best)

½ teaspoon basil (fresh is best)

Salt and pepper, to taste

1. Add three eggs to a small saucepan filled with water. Place over high heat and boil for 15 minutes.
2. Remove eggs from boiling water and place in a bowl of cold water. Cool eggs until easy to handle.
3. Peel and chop eggs and add to a large bowl. Add the rest of the ingredients to the bowl and mix well.

Summer Squash Pancakes (makes 6 to 7 pancakes)

1 small zucchini, shredded

1 small yellow squash, shredded

1 small carrot, shredded

½ yellow onion, shredded

1 cup almond flour/meal

2 eggs

2 garlic cloves, minced

1 teaspoon dried basil

1 teaspoon dried parsley

Salt and pepper, to taste

2 tablespoons fat of choice (I prefer pastured butter)

½ avocado, diced (to garnish)

½ green onion, diced (to garnish)

1. In a large bowl, mix together with your hands the vegetables, almond flour, eggs, garlic, basil, parsley, and salt and pepper.
2. Make six to seven patties.
3. Heat a large skillet over medium-high heat. Add fat of choice (I usually use pastured butter). Place patties in the pan—be careful of overcrowding—and cook for five to seven minutes on each side, until pancakes are browned.
4. Remove from heat and serve topped with avocado and green onions.

Check out YesICanGetPregnant.com for more recipes!

Notes

Chapter One

p. 7: *The widely cited statistic that one in three women ages 35 to 39...* Twenge, J. "How Long Can You Wait to Have a Baby." *The Atlantic* (June 2013): www.theatlantic.com/magazine/archive/2013/07/how-long-can-you-wait-to-have-a-baby/309374.

p. 7: *In fact, of the more recent studies on age and fertility...* Dunson, DB, Baird, DD, Colombo, B. "Increased Infertility with Age in Men and Women." *Obstetrics & Gynecology*, 103, no.1 (January 2004): 51–56.

p. 7: *Another study in 2013 out of the journal* Fertility and Sterility... Rothman KJ, Wise LA, Sørensen HT, Riis AH, Mikkelsen EM, Hatch EE. "Volitional Determinants and Age-Related Decline in Fecundability: A General Population Prospective Cohort Study in Denmark." *Fertility and Sterililty* 99, no. 7 (June 2013): 1958– 1964.

Chapter Two

p. 32: *In fact, one study published by the journal* Archives of Sexual Behavior... Levin, RJ. "The Physiology of Sexual Arousal in the Human Female: A Recreational and Procreational Synthesis." *Archives of Sexual Behavior* 31, no. 5 (2002): 405–411.

p. 38: *Enviromental Toxins and Our Fertility...* The American College of Obstetricians and Gynecologists. "Environmental Chemicals Harm Reproductive Health." (2013): www.acog.org/About_ACOG/News_Room/News_Releases/2013/Environmental_Chemicals_Harm_Reproductive_Health.

Chapter Three

p. 44: *In 2010,* Frontiers in Endocrinology *published...* Zama, AM, Uzumco, M. "Epigenetic Effects of Endocrine-Disrupting Chemicals on Female Reproduction: An Ovarian Perspective." *Frontiers in Neuroendocrinology* 31, no. 4 (October 2010): 420–439.

p. 44: *Another study, published by the* American Journal of Physiology, Endocrinology... Herod, SM, Dettmer AM, Novak, MA, Meyer, JS, Cameron, JL. "Sensitivity to Stress-Induced Reproductive Dysfunction Is Associated with a Selective but Not a Generalized Increase in Activity of the Adrenal Axis." *American Journal of Physiology, Endocrinology and Metabolism* 300, no. 1 (January 2011): E28–E36.

p. 45: An article from Proceedings of the National Academy of Sciences... Epel ES, Blackburn EH, Lin J, Dhabhar FS, Adler NE, Morrow JD, Cawthon RM. "Accelerated Telomere Shortening in Response to Life Stress." *Proceedings of the National Academy of Sciences of the United States of America* 101, no. 49 (December 2004): 17312–17315.

p. 45: *Another paper, published by* Human Genetics *in 2012, discusses...* Cortessis, VK, Duncan CT, Levine, JA, Breton, CV, Mack, TM, Siegmund, KD, Haile, RW, Laird, PW. "Environmental Epigenetics: Prospects for Studying Epigenetic Mediation of Exposure–Response Relationships." *Human Genetics* 131, no. 10 (October 2012): 1565–1589.

p. 49: *A 2012 review of current research on this topic...* Haller-Kikkatalo, K, Salumets, A, Uibo, R. "Review on Autoimmune Reactions in Female Infertility: Antibodies to Follicle Stimulating Hormone." *Clinical and Developmental Immunology* (2012): http://dx.doi.org/10.1155/2012/762541.

p. 50: *Recent research published in the journals* Gynecological Endocrinology... Abalovich, M, Mitelberg, L, Allami, C, Guitierrez, S, Alcaraz, G, Otero, P, Levalle, O. "Subclinical Hypothyroidism and Thyroid Autoimmunity in Women with Infertility." *Gynecological Endocrinology* 23, no. 5 (May 2007): 279–283.

Gerhard, I, Becker, T, Eggert-Kruse, W, Klinga, K, Bunnebaum, B. *"Thyroid and Ovarian Function in Infertile Women." Human Reproduction* 6, no. 3 (1991): 338–345.

p. 51: *Additionally, a study published by* The European Journal of Endocrinology... Ganie, MA, Marwaha, RK, Aggarwal, R, Singh, S. "High Prevalence of Polycystic Ovary Syndrome Characteristics in Girls with Euthyroid Chronic Lymphocytic Thyroiditis: A Case–Control Study." *European Journal of Endocrinology* 162 (2010): 1117–1122.

p. 51: Polish Endocrinology *published a paper in 2012 concluding that CD...* Miskiewicz, P, Kepczynska-Nyk, A, Bednarczuk, T. "Coeliac Disease in Endocrine Diseases of Autoimmune Origin." *Polish Endocrinology* 63, no. 3 (2012): 240–249.

p. 51: *Dr. Sheila Crowe, a professor at the University of Virginia, spoke with* The New York Times... Crowe, S. "Can Foods Contribute to Infertility?" *New York Times* (February 3, 2010).

p. 51: *Virginia T. Ladd, President and Executive Director of the American Autoimmune Related Diseases Association (AARDA) stated...* Rattue, G. "Autoimmune Disease Rates Increases." *Medical News Today* (June 22, 2012): www.medicalnewstoday.com/articles/246960.php.

p. 55: *In 2009, the journal* Seminars in Reproductive Medicine... Dupont, C, Brenner, CA, Armant, DR. "Epigenetics: Definition, Mechanisms and Clinical Perspective." *Seminars in Reproductive Medicine* 27, no. 5 (September 2009): 351–357.

p. 55: *Another research article published in a 2013 issue of* Cell Metabolism... Tilly, JA, Sinclair, DA. "Germline Energetics, Aging, and Female Infertility." *Cell Metabolism* 17, no. 6 (2013): http://onlinedigeditions.com/display_article.php?id=1428338.

Chapter Four

p. 63: *In 2013, the* International Journal of Environmental Research and Public Health... Keniger, LE, Gaston, KJ, Irvine, KN, Fuller, RA. "What Are the Benefits of Interacting with Nature?" *International Journal of Environmental Research and Public Health* 10, no. 3 (March 2013): 913–935.

p. 63: *Research published in Oxford's* Health Promotion International... Maller, C, Townsend, M, Pryor, A, Brown, P, St. Leger, L. "Healthy Nature Healthy People: 'Contact with Nature' as an Upstream Health Promotion Intervention for Populations." *Health Promotion International* 21, no. 1 (March 2006): 45–54.

p. 63: *Another publication,* The Experience of Nature... Kaplan, R, Kaplan, S. *The Experience of Nature: A Psychological Perspective.* New York: Cambridge University Press, 1989.

p. 65: *There is some evidence that before the age of artificial lighting...* Kittel, M, Metzger, D. "Make the Most of Sleep and Sunlight: How Fertility Is Affected by Sleep and Sunlight," About.com (October 2004). Reprinted from: *Stay Fertile Longer: Everything You Need to Know to Get Pregnant Now — Or Whenever You're Ready* by Mary Kittel with Deborah Metzger, MD, PhD © 2004 by Rodale, Inc.: http://womenshealth.about.com/od/pregnancyrelatedissues/a/sleepsunlight.htm.

p. 67: *Science shows that indoor plants boost moods, reduce anxiety...* Chang, CY, Chen, PK. "Human Response to Window Views and Indoor Plants in the Workplace." *HortScience* 40, no. 5 (August 2005): 1354–1359.

Chapter Five

p. 76: *Recent scientific research, presented at the Annual Clinical Meeting...* The American College of Obstetricians and Gynecologists. "High Protein, Low Carb Diets Greatly Improve Fertility" (May 2013): www.acog.org/About_ACOG/News_Room/News_Releases/2013/High_Protein_Low_Carb_Diets_Greatly_Improve_Fertility.

p. 76: *As well, research out of Harvard University has shown that full-fat...* Chavarro JE, Rich-Edwards JW, Rosner BA, Willett WC. "Diet and

Lifestyle in the Prevention of Ovulatory Disorder Infertility." *Obstetrics and Gynecology* 110, no. 5 (November 2007): 1050–1058.

p. 76: *Several scientific articles have shown that antioxidants...* Ruder, EH, Hartman, TJ, Blumberg, J, Goldman, MB. "Oxidative Stress and Antioxidants: Exposure and Impact on Female Fertility." *Human Reprodcution Update* 14, no. 4 (July–August 2008): 345–357.

Ruder, EH, Terryl, J, Hartman, B, Goldmanc, MB. *Impact of Oxidative Stress on Female Fertility. Current Opinion in Obstetrics and Gynecology* 21, no. 3 (June 2009): 219–222.

p. 76: *In addition, other research has directly linked pesticides...* Orton, F, Rosivatz, E, Scholze, M, Kortenkamp, A. "Widely Used Pesticides with Previously Unknown Endocrine Activity Revealed as in vitro Antiandrogens." *Environmental Health Perspectives* 119, no. 6 (June 2011): 794–800.

p. 76: *and in animal studies, the dietary intake of genetically modified foods...* Dean, A, Armstrong, J. "Genetically Modified Foods." *American Academy of Environmental Medicine* (2009): www.aaemonline.org/gmopost.html.

p. 78: *Several research articles published in prestigious journals...* Choi, JM, Lebwohl, B, Wang, J, Lee, SK, Murray, JA, Sauer, MV, Green, PH. "Increased Prevalence of Celiac Disease in Patients with Unexplained Infertility in the United States." *The Journal of Reproductive Medicine* 56, no. 5–6 (May–June 2011): 199–203.

Khoshbaten, M, Rostami, NM, Farzady, L, Sharifi, N, Hashemi, SH, Rostami, K. *"Fertility Disorder Associated with Celiac Disease in Males and Females: Fact or Fiction?" The Journal of Obstetrics and Gynecology Research* 37, no. 10 (October 2011): 1308–1312.

Kumar, A, Meena, M, Begum, N, Kuman, N, Gupta, RK, Aggarwal, S, Prasad, S, Batra, S. *Latent Celiac Disease in Reproductive Performance of Women. Fertility and Sterility* 95, no. 3 (March 2011): 922–927.

p. 80: *According to the* American Academy of Environmental Medicine... Dean, A, Armstrong, J. "Genetically Modified Foods." *American Academy of Environmental Medicine* (2009): www.aaemonline.org/gmopost.html.

p. 80: *According to Jeffrey Smith, a leading national expert on the dangers of genetically modified organisms...* Karlin, M. "Monsanto and Genetically Engineered Food: Playing Roulette with Our Health." *Truth-Out* (November 13, 2012): http://truth-out.org/news/item/12715-monsanto-and-genetically-engineered-food-playing-roulette-with-our-health.

p. 81: The American Journal of Clinical Nutrition *published a study...* Cassidy, A, Bingham, S, Setchell, KD. "Biological Effects of a Diet of Soy Protein Rich in Isoflavones on the Menstrual Cycle of Premenopausal Women." *The American Journal of Clinical Nutrition* 60, no. 3 (September 1994): 333–340.

p. 81: *irregular menstruation for three months following the cessation...* Trum-Hunter, B. "The Downside of Soybean Consumption." *The American Nutrition Association* (2001): http://americannutrition-association.org/newsletter/downside-soybeanconsumption.

p. 82: *Scientists at Harvard have shown that following a low-sugar diet...* Chavarro, JE, Rich-Edwards, JW, Rosner, BA, Willett, WC. "Diet and Lifestyle in the Prevention of Ovulatory Disorder Infertility." *Obstetrics and Gynecology* 110, no. 5 (November 2007): 1050–1058.

p. 83: *In 2013, the journal* Obstetrics and Gynecology... Committee Opinion No. 575. American College of Obstetricians and Gynecologists. "Exposure to Toxic Environmental Agents." *Obstetrics and Gynecology* 122 (2013): 931–935.

p. 83: *These substances are chemically derived and have been scientifically shown...* Whitehouse, CR, Boullata, J, McCauley, LA. "The Potential Toxicity of Artificial Sweeteners." *American Association of Occupational Health and Nurses* 56, no. 6 (June 2008): 251–259.

Bandyopadhyay, A, Ghoshal, S, Mukherjee, A. "Genotoxicity Testing of Low-Calorie Sweeteners: Aspartame, Acesulfame-K, and Saccharin." *Drug and Chemical Toxicology* 31, no. 4(2008): 447–457.

Chapter Six

p. 99: *In 2010, the journal* Frontiers in Neuroendocrinology *published a paper...* Zama, AM, Uzumcu, M. "Epigenetic Effects of

Endocrine-Disrupting Chemicals on Female Reproduction: An Ovarian Perspective." *Frontiers in Neuroendocrinology* 31, no. 4 (October 2010): 420–439.

p. 99: *Another research paper published in 2009 by the journal...* Vandenberg, LN. Maffini, MV, Sonnenschein, C, Rubin, BS, Soto AM. "Bisphenol-A and the Great Divide: A Review of Controversies in the Field of Endocrine Disruption." *Endocrine Reviews* 30, no. 1 (February 2009): 75–95.

Chapter Seven

p. 106: *In fact, research out of the journal* Fertility and Sterility, *based on...* Klonoff-Cohen, H, Chu, E, Nataraian, L, Sieber, W. "A prospective study of stress among women undergoing in vitro fertilization or gamete intrafallopian transfer." *Fertility and Sterility* 76, no. 4 (October 2001): 675–687.

p. 106: *In another study published in the same journal, researchers found...* Demyttenaere K, Bonte L, Gheldof M, Veraeke M, Meuleman C, Vanderschuerem D. "Coping Style and Depression Level Influence Outcome in vitro Fertilization." *Fertility and Sterility* 69 (1998): 1026–1033.

p. 124: *A very impressive study out of the Mind–Body Medicine Institute...* Domar, A, Clapp, D, Slawsby, E, Dusek, J, Kessel, B, Freizinger, M. "Impact of Group Psychological Interventions on Pregnancy Rates in Infertile Women." *Fertility and Sterility* 73, no.4 (April 2000): 805–811.

p. 124: *Women who meditated...* Domar, A, Seibel, M, Benson, H. "The Mind/Body Program for Infertility: A New Treatment Program for Women with Infertility." *Fertility and Sterility* 53 (1990): 246–249.

p. 126: *Research out of the Benson–Henry Institute...* Bhasin, MK, Dusek, JA, Chang, BH, Joseph, MG, Denninger, JW, Fricchione, GL, Benson, H, Libermann, TA. "Relaxation Response Induces Temporal Transcriptome Changes in Energy Metabolism, Insulin Secretion, and Inflammatory Pathways." *PLoS ONE* 8, no 5 (May 2013): doi: 10.1371/journal.pone.0062817.

p. 127: *study published in the* Journal of Clinical Endocrinology & Metabolism... Kim, SH, Schneider, SM, Bevans, M, Kravitz, L, Mermier, C, Quails, C, Burge, MR. "PTSD Symptom Reduction with Mindfulness-Based Stretching and Deep Breathing Exercise: Randomized Controlled Clinical Trial of Efficacy." *Journal of Clinical Endocrinology and Metabolism* 98, no. 7 (July 2013): 2984–2992.

Chapter Nine

p. 150: *Several articles have been published in the scientific journal* Fertility and Sterility... Chang R, Chung PH, Rosenwaks Z. "Role of Acupuncture in the Treatment of Female Infertility." *Fertility and Sterility* 78, no 6 (December 2002): 1149–1153.

Ng EH, So WS, Gao J, Wong YY, Ho PC. *The Role of Acupuncture in the Management of Subfertility. Fertility and Sterility* 90, no. 1 (July 2008): 1–13.

Westergaard, LG, Mao, Q, Krogslund, M, Sandrini, S, Lenz, S, Grinsted, J. *"Acupuncture on the Day of Embryo Transfer Significantly Improves the Reproductive Outcome in Infertile Women: A Prospective, Randomized Trial." Fertility and Sterility* 85, no. 5 (May 2006): 1341–1346.

Chapter Ten

p. 157: *however, recent research published in 2007...* Ali, AFM, Fateen, B, Ezzet, A, Ramadan, A, Badawy, H, El-Tobge, A. "Polycystic Ovary Syndrome as an Autoimmune Disease: A New Concept." *Obstetrics and Gynecology* 94, no.4 (April 2000): S48.

p. 158: *Birth Control and Ovulation...* Jain, T, Resslet, IB. "Reversible Contraception: Does It Affect Future Fertility?" *Contemporary Ob/Gyn* (September 1, 2010): http://contemporaryobgyn .modernmedicine.com/contemporary-obgyn/news/modernmedicine/modern-medicine-now/reversible-contraception-does-it-affect-f?id=&sk=&date=&%0A%09%09%09&pageID=3#.

p. 161: *Furthermore, endometriosis shares similarities with several autoimmune diseases...* Eisenber, VH, Zolti, M, Soriano, D. "Is There an Association Between Autoimmunity and Endometriosis?" *Autoimmunity Reviews* 11, no. 11 (September 2012): 806–814.

p. 161: *in the journal* Fertility and Sterility *concluded that...* Nothnick, WB. "Treating Endometriosis as an Autoimmune Disease." *Fertility and Sterility* 76, no. 2 (August 2001): 223–231.

Acknowledgments

There is just so much to be thankful for. There is so much in this life of mine to appreciate and I am gushing with gratitude. Thank YOU.

Of course, first and foremost, thank you to my magnificent parents. Without their undying love, friendship, and guidance none of this would be possible. To my mommy—you are my sunshine, my ultimate role model, and my best friend. To my daddy—for always standing by my side, being my biggest fan, my bestest friend, and keeping me wrapped in the warm blanket of your love all the way from heaven. It is a privilege to be your daughter. You are with me always. Every day I shine for you.

To my brother Harry, I love you and I am so proud to call you my family and my friend. To my Lily—I love you so much. Thank you for your strength and friendship. To my lovebugs Sam and Ryan—you have my heart, and watching you grow fills me with joy like nothing else can.

A special thanks to my dear loves. Not a day goes by that I'm not grateful for each of you (even if I'm terrible at picking up the phone to call): Auntie, Uncle Ed, Aunt Eileen, Uncle Jim, Blaguna, Uncle Mike, Aunt Dawn, Uncle Tom, Aunt Carolyn, Uncle Frank, Aunt Marilyn, Uncle Monroe. Thank you always for your unwavering love and support. I am so grateful for all of you.

To my beloved friends: Melanie Vangopoulos, Nathalie Brochu, Hima Katari, Brooke Thorburn, Heather Kreutter, Javi Ruiz, Jolie

Curtsinger-Schwartz, Danielle Quintana, Johanna Berry-Wasser, Kimmy Holmstrom, Jessica Diamond-Meincke, Siobhan Carpenter, Athena Still, Rossana Parrotta, Kymberly Kelly, Sarah Coles Mckeown, Katie Chatzopoulos, Ali Johnson, Megan Driscoll, Sasha Weiss, Piper Weiss, and John Sadowski—the joy, laughter, love, and inspiration we share fills me up. I love you to the moon and back. I am beyond thankful for each and every one of you and for your relentless love, support, and friendship.

To Jon Garbo—you are my beacon and the best coach, friend, and cheerleader anyone could ask for.

To Sloane Miller—your feedback, friendship, and fire always bring out my best and I love you like mad because of it.

To Anner Bohner—my brilliant, determined, and devoted agent and friend. Thank you (and Jeff) for being a part of this journey.

To Julia Pastore—your wisdom and insight helped bring this book to fruition. Thank you for believing in my mission.

To all of those who have come to me for guidance, direction, and healing, and to those of you who have guided, healed, and taught me—without you, none of this would be possible. Thank YOU for sharing your life with me. My world is a better place for having each of you in it.

To the love and light that surrounds me each and every day—thank you for always having my back and encouraging me to continuously find joy and love in all that comes my way. This is a good life and I look forward to more, more, more!!

Index

About the Author

Acupuncturist, herbalist, and author Aimee Raupp is a women's health and fertility expert. Her mission is to educate and inspire women to improve their health, celebrate their beauty, prevent disease, and increase their fertility so they can live full, self-directed lives and achieve on their own terms.

In her 20s, working as a research scientist in the field of neurobiology, Raupp struggled with ongoing health care issues. When Western medicine was unable to provide relief, she turned to Eastern medicine. From this early experience as a patient of acupuncture, she discovered how a mind–body–nutrition approach was key to finally overcoming her illnesses and maintaining good health. Ever since, Raupp has dedicated her life to the practice of Traditional Oriental Medicine.

Raupp's first book, *Chill Out and Get Healthy* (Penguin), is a call-to-arms for women to reclaim their emotional and physical wellness before lack of wellness becomes serious, intractable disease. Her inspiration for the book came from her many female patients in their 20s, 30s, and 40s, from all walks of life, often with successful and dynamic careers, who faced all-too-common illnesses that result from high-stakes, fast-paced living.

Raupp is currently in private practice in Manhattan, the Hamptons, and Nyack, NY, and has developed her own original, organic, gluten-free, and vegan Aimee Raupp Beauty product line.

She has appeared on ABC Television's *The View*, Yahoo! Shine, Martha Stewart Radio, FOX Television's *Good Day New York*, and in national magazines *Glamour*, *Woman's Day*, *Self*, and *Better Nutrition*. She has served as a spokesperson for such brands and companies as Culturelle, Whole Foods, lululemon athletica, and the American Leisure Spa Group. She is the women's health columnist for *Acupuncture Today*, a monthly contributor to Mommybites.com, and an active blogger.

Raupp earned a Master's of Science degree in Traditional Oriental Medicine from the Pacific College of Oriental Medicine in San Diego, California, and a Bachelor's degree in biology from Rutgers University in New Brunswick, New Jersey. She holds a license in acupuncture and Chinese herbology in the state of New York and is certified by the National Certification Commission for Acupuncture and Oriental Medicine.

For more information, visit www.YesICanGetPregnant.com